Teriyaki

Discover A Japanese Sauce that Change Your Cooking: A Teriyaki Cookbook with Delicious Teriyaki Recipes

By
BookSumo Press
All rights reserved

Published by
http://www.booksumo.com

Table of Contents

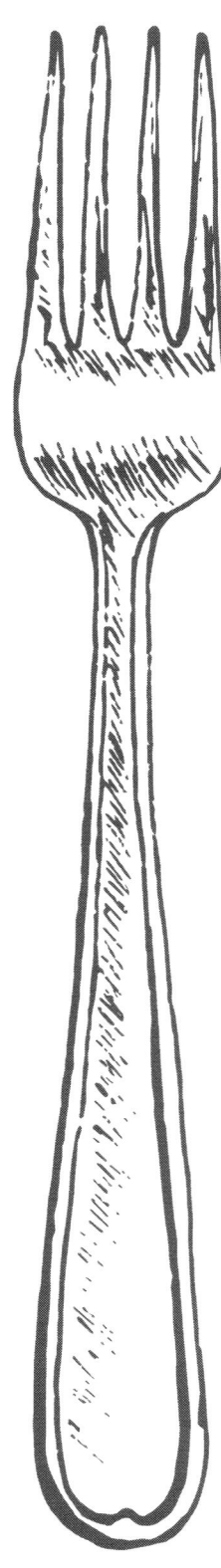

Classic Teriyaki Sauce 7

Homemade Japanese House Jerky 8

Classic Teriyaki Chuck Burgers 9

Japanese Chicken Legs 10

Teriyaki Florets Bowls 11

Teriyaki Chicken Thighs 12

Sweet Teriyaki Spuds 13

Tuesday's Steak 14

Teriyaki Penne 15

Tropical Teriyaki Kabobs 16

Teriyaki Steak BBQ 17

Teriyaki Beef Sandwiches 18

Glazed Asparagus Salad 19

Kiki's Honey Salmon 20

Tex Mex Teriyaki Steak 21

5-Ingredient Teriyaki Sauce 22

Hibachi Tofu 23

Everything Teriyaki Dinner 24

Sticky Ginger Meatballs 25

Teriyaki Bean Pods 26

Kyoto Fish Kabobs 27

My First Teriyaki Sauce 28

Japanese House Quinoa 29

60-Minute Japanese Pilaf 30

Big World Burgers 31

Teriyaki Orzo 32

Tilapia Japan 33

Teriyaki Stir Fried Veggies 34

Orange Fish 35

Simple Ginger Teriyaki Salad 36

Teriyaki Rice Cakes 37

Summer Teriyaki BBQ 38

Teriyaki Slaw 39

Teriyaki Pasta Salad 40

Homemade Teriyaki Chips 41

Bella Burger Teriyaki 42

Sticky Chicken 43

Egg Noodle Teriyaki 44

Full Mango Skillet 45

Wild Rice Teriyaki 46

Teriyaki Seafood Skewers 47

Teriyaki Pasta 48

Teriyaki Cod 49

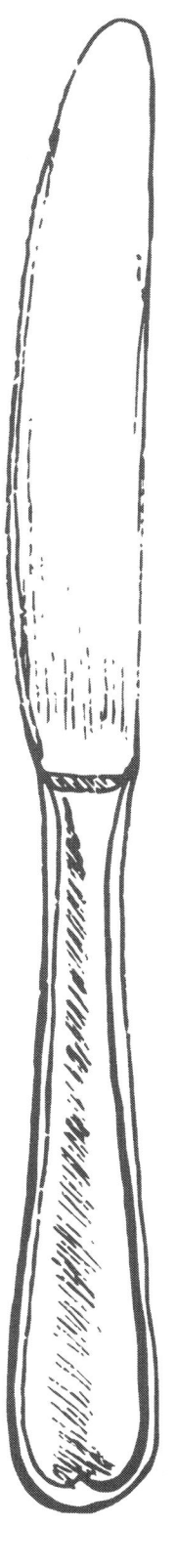

Vegetarian Teriyaki Skillet 50

Teriyaki Backyard Burgers 51

Sushi Chisaka 52

How to Make Teriyaki Sauce 53

Asian Fusion Chicken Wings 54

Teriyaki Spaghetti Squash 55

West Indian Teriyaki Fish 56

Teriyaki Burritos 57

Teriyaki Beef 58

Mediterranean Meets Japanese Skillet 59

Mushroom Teriyaki 60

Korean Dinner 61

Thursday's Japanese Meatloaf Teriyaki 62

Braised Green Been Skillet 63

Yuki's Fish Cakes Teriyaki 64

Tofu Teriyaki 65

Hibachi Filets 66

Teriyaki Cauliflower Bowls 67

Teriyaki Sirloin 68

Waldorf Teriyaki 69

Sakura's 6-Ingredient Cutlets 70

Louisiana x Japanese Teriyaki 71

White Fish Teriyaki 72

Teriyaki Brasileiro 73

Teriyaki London Broil 74

Teriyaki Lunch Box 75

Topped Teriyaki Chicken Breasts 76

Teriyaki Meat Brine 77

Shenzhen Stir Fry 78

Weeknight Burger Teriyaki 79

Teriyaki Meatball Sampler 80

Alaskan Teriyaki 81

Country Vegetable Teriyaki 82

Mr. Chow's Teriyaki Burgers 83

Linguine Teriyaki 84

Sesame Salmon 85

Teriyaki Seafood Bowls 86

Teriyaki Noodles 87

Chicken Wing Teriyaki 88

Caribbean Teriyaki Sliders 89

Teriyaki Pasta Salad 90

Spicy Japanese Pizza 92

Ginger Teriyaki Nuts 93

Teriyaki Oysters 94

Hawaiian Teriyaki Ribs 95

Mushroom Teriyaki 96

Beef Teriyaki 97

20 Minute Weeknight Teriyaki Fish 98

Classic Teriyaki Sauce

Prep Time: 10 mins
Total Time: 25 mins

Servings per Recipe: 1
Calories   133.4
Fat   0.0g
Cholesterol   0.0mg
Sodium   2062.3mg
Carbohydrates   30.1g
Protein   4.0g

Ingredients

1/4 C. tamari soy sauce
1 C. water
freshly grated ginger
3 tbsps brown sugar
1 minced garlic clove

2 tbsps cornstarch
1/4 C. cold water

Directions

1. Place a saucepan over medium heat. Stir in it 1 C. water, tamari, brown sugar, garlic, and ginger.
2. Cook them until they start boiling while stirring all the time.
3. Get a mixing bowl: Whisk in it the cornstarch with 1/4 C. of water.
4. Add it to the saucepan and keep whisking it until it becomes thick.
5. Adjust the seasoning of your teriyaki sauce then serve it.
6. Enjoy.

HOMEMADE
Japanese House Jerky

Prep Time: 20 mins
Total Time: 6 hrs 20 mins

Servings per Recipe: 1
Calories   2020.0
Fat   71.1g
Cholesterol   612.3mg
Sodium   15416.4mg
Carbohydrates   105.0g
Protein   228.3g

Ingredients

- 5 lbs. beef flank steaks
- 2 C. Worcestershire sauce
- 1 1/2 C. teriyaki sauce
- 3 tsps liquid smoke
- 1 C. soy sauce
- 4 tsps onion powder
- 2 tsps garlic powder
- 1 tsp cayenne powder
- 4 tsps black pepper
- 1 tbsp sea salt
- 1 1/4 tbsps red pepper flakes
- 4 tbsps brown sugar
- 2 tbsps honey
- 1 tbsp maple syrup
- 3 bamboo skewers
- aluminum foil

Directions

1. Place the beef steaks on a baking tray. Place them in the freezer for 25 min. Get a large mixing bowl: Mix in it the remaining ingredients to make the marinade.
2. Place the steaks on a cutting board and slice them into 1/8 to 1/4 inch slices. Discard the fat from them.
3. Add the steaks to the teriyaki marinade and mix them well. Place it in the fridge overnight.
4. Use paper towels to pat the jerky slices dry. Thread them onto skewers. Arrange them on the middle oven rack after greasing it. Place a sheet of foil in the bottom to catch the drippings.
5. Turn the oven to the lowest setting. Adjust the door so it can stay slightly open.
6. Let them cook for 6 h until they become dry.
7. Allow your jerky beef to cool down completely then pack it into sterilized jars.
8. Enjoy.

Classic Teriyaki Chuck Burgers

Prep Time: 15 mins
Total Time: 25 mins

Servings per Recipe: 6
Calories   517.5
Fat   27.7g
Cholesterol   104.3mg
Sodium   1157.1mg
Carbohydrates   34.1g
Protein   31.7g

Ingredients

1/4 C. soy sauce
1/4 C. honey
2 cloves garlic, pressed
1 tsp ginger
1/3 C. mayonnaise

2 lbs. ground chuck
1/2 tsp salt
1/4 tsp pepper
6 hamburger buns

Directions

1. Before you do anything, preheat the grill and grease it.
2. Get a mixing bowl: Whisk in it the soy sauce with honey, garlic, and ginger.
3. Get a small mixing bowl: Whisk in it 2 tsp of the honey mixture with mayo. Place it aside.
4. Add the beef with salt, and pepper to the remaining honey mixture. Mix them well.
5. Shape the mixture into 6 patties. Coat them with a cooking spray.
6. Place them on the grill and let them cook for 3 to 4 min on each side.
7. Assemble your burgers with toppings of your choice then serve them warm.
8. Enjoy.

JAPANESE
Chicken Legs

Prep Time: 10 mins
Total Time: 40 mins

Servings per Recipe: 4
Calories 576.7
Fat 22.8g
Cholesterol 118.2mg
Sodium 4160.4mg
Carbohydrates 57.9g
Protein 35.7g

Ingredients

8 -12 chicken drumsticks
1 C. soy sauce
1 C. brown sugar, packed
1 C. water
3 tbsps olive oil
1 tsp ginger

Directions

1. Place a pot over high heat. Heat in it the oil. Cook in it the drumsticks until they become golden brown.
2. Get a mixing bowl: Whisk in it the soy sauce with sugar, water, ginger, a pinch of salt and pepper.
3. Pour the mixture over the chicken drumsticks. Cook them until they start boiling.
4. Lower the heat and let them cook for 25 min until the chicken drumsticks are done.
5. Serve your sticky and glazed drumsticks warm with some rice or lettuce.
6. Enjoy.

Teriyaki Florets Bowls

🥣 Prep Time: 8 mins
🕐 Total Time: 20 mins

Servings per Recipe: 4
Calories   50.9
Fat   0.4g
Cholesterol   0.0mg
Sodium   214.2mg
Carbohydrates 9.9g
Protein   3.9g

Ingredients

17.5 oz. broccoli, cut into florets, rinsed and drained
4 garlic cloves, chopped
1 tbsp teriyaki sauce
fresh ground black pepper

olive oil flavored cooking spray

Directions

1. Before you do anything, preheat the oven to 400 F.
2. Get a large mixing bowl: Toss in it the broccoli with garlic, teriyaki sauce, a pinch of salt and pepper.
3. Grease a baking sheet with some oil. Spread in it the broccoli florets.
4. Cook them in the oven for 7 min. Serve it warm.
5. Enjoy.

TERIYAKI
Chicken Thighs

🥘 Prep Time: 15 mins
🕒 Total Time: 30 mins

Servings per Recipe: 4
Calories   242.3
Fat   8.2g
Cholesterol   115.0mg
Sodium   1047.3mg
Carbohydrates   11.9g
Protein   28.9g

Ingredients

Marinade
1/4 C. ketchup
1/4 C. hoisin sauce
2 tbsps soy sauce
2 tbsps rice vinegar
2 tsps garlic, minced
2 tsps ginger, minced

2 tsps dark sesame oil
Chicken
8 boneless skinless chicken thighs
sesame seeds, toasted in a skillet
cooked rice
green onion top, cut into strips

Directions

1. Get a mixing bowl: Whisk in it all the marinade ingredients.
2. Place the chicken thighs in a zip lock bag. Pour over it the marinade.
3. Seal the bag and shake it to coat. Let them marinade for 5 h.
4. Before you do anything, preheat the grill and grease it.
5. Drain the chicken thighs and grill them for 6 to 7 min on each side.
6. Garnish them with some sesame seeds and green onion. Serve them warm.
7. Enjoy.

Sweet Teriyaki Spuds

Prep Time: 10 mins
Total Time: 26 mins

Servings per Recipe: 5
Calories	129.9
Fat	2.4g
Cholesterol	6.1mg
Sodium	166.5mg
Carbohydrates	24.7g
Protein	3.0g

Ingredients

- 1 1/2 lbs. red skinned small potatoes, quartered
- 1 tbsp butter, cut into pieces
- 1 tbsp bottled teriyaki sauce
- 1/4 tsp garlic salt
- 1/4 tsp Italian seasoning, crushed
- 1 dash black pepper
- 1 dash cayenne pepper
- 1 tsp rosemary, minced
- sour cream

Directions

1. Get a microwave safe pan. Toss in it the potatoes with the remaining ingredients.
2. Microwave it for 16 min on high. Serve it warm as a side dish.
3. Enjoy.

TUESDAY'S
Steak

🍳 Prep Time: 15 mins
🕐 Total Time: 20 mins

Servings per Recipe: 2
Calories			179.3
Fat				13.6g
Cholesterol		0.0mg
Sodium			1099.3mg
Carbohydrates		9.9g
Protein			2.5g

Ingredients

1 - 2 onion, sliced into rings
1 piece eye steak fillet
1 tbsp sake
2 tbsps rice vinegar
2 tbsps soy sauce
1 tsp sugar
salt

2 tbsps oil, divided
steamed rice

Directions

1. Season the steak with some salt and pepper.
2. Place a pan over medium heat. Heat in it 1 tbsp of oil. Cook in it the onion for 3 min.
3. Drain it and place it aside. Add the remaining oil to the pan and heat it.
4. Cook in it the steak for 3 to 5 min on each side. Drain it and place it aside.
5. Lower the heat and stir the sake into the skillet. Let it cook for 20 sec.
6. Stir in the rice vinegar with soy sauce, sugar and a pinch of salt. Cook them for 1 min.
7. Place the steak on a serving plate and top it with the onion.
8. Drizzle the teriyaki sauce on top then serve it immediately.
9. Enjoy.

Teriyaki Penne

Prep Time: 5 mins
Total Time: 15 mins

Servings per Recipe: 6
Calories   189.1
Fat   3.3g
Cholesterol   0.0mg
Sodium   478.0mg
Carbohydrates   36.2g
Protein   5.6g

Ingredients

- 8 ounces penne pasta
- 1/2 tsp grated ginger
- 1 clove garlic, minced
- 1 tbsp toasted sesame oil
- 3 C. broccoli slaw mix
- 2 C. sliced fresh mushrooms
- 1/4 C. teriyaki sauce
- 1/4 C. sliced green onion

Directions

1. Prepare the pasta by following the instructions on the package. Drain it.
2. Place a large pan over medium heat. Heat in it the oil. Cook in it the ginger for 10 sec.
3. Add the broccoli with teriyaki sauce and mushrooms. Season them with a pinch of salt and pepper.
4. Let them cook for 6 min. Add the pasta and stir them to coat.
5. Serve your teriyaki slaw salad warm.
6. Enjoy.

TROPICAL
Teriyaki Kabobs

Prep Time: 15 mins
Total Time: 20 mins

Servings per Recipe: 4
Calories   931.9
Fat   82.8g
Cholesterol   112.3mg
Sodium   2046.7mg
Carbohydrates   34.4g
Protein   13.8g

Ingredients

1 lb. beef, cubed
1 (16 ounce) cans pineapple chunks in juice
1/2 C. soy sauce
1/4 C. brown sugar
2 garlic cloves, minced
1/2 tsp minced ginger
1/2 tsp sliced lemongrass
1/4 C. sliced scallion
2 tsps sesame oil

Directions

1. Get a large zip lock bag: Place in it all the ingredients and seal it.
2. Shake it to coat them. Place it in the fridge for 3 h.
3. Before you do anything, preheat the grill and grease it.
4. Drain the beef and pineapple chunks from the marinade. Thread them while alternating between them onto skewers.
5. Grill them for 4 to 6 min on each side. Serve them warm.
6. Enjoy.

Teriyaki Steak BBQ

Prep Time: 15 mins
Total Time: 25 mins

Servings per Recipe: 6
Calories   238.2
Fat   9.4g
Cholesterol   68.0mg
Sodium   962.5mg
Carbohydrates   9.6g
Protein   28.7g

Ingredients

1/3 C. soy sauce
2 tbsps vegetable oil
1 tbsp brown sugar
1 garlic clove, minced
1 tsp ground ginger
1 tsp seasoning salt
1 1/2 lbs. boneless sirloin steaks, cubed

12 fresh mushrooms
1 large green pepper, cut into pieces
1 large onion, cut into wedges
12 cherry tomatoes

Directions

1. Get a mixing bowl: Mix in it the soy sauce, oil, brown sugar, garlic, ginger, and salt to make the marinade.
2. Get a large zip lock bag. Place in it the beef slices and pour over the marinade.
3. Seal the bag and shake it to coat. Place it in the fridge and let it sit overnight.
4. Before you do anything, preheat the grill and grease it.
5. Drain the beef dices and thread along with cherry tomatoes, green pepper, onion, and mushrooms onto skewers.
6. Grill them for 5 to 7 min on each side while basting them with the remaining marinade.
7. Serve your kabobs warm with some pita bread.
8. Enjoy.

TERIYAKI
Beef Sandwiches

Prep Time: 15 mins
Total Time: 17 mins

Servings per Recipe: 3
Calories   741.1
Fat   43.9g
Cholesterol   138.3mg
Sodium   1306.7mg
Carbohydrates   30.1g
Protein   54.9g

Ingredients

4 C. coleslaw mix
3 tbsps chopped parsley
2 tbsps rice vinegar
2 tbsps vegetable oil
2 tbsps light sesame oil
3/4 tsp ginger
1 1/2 lbs. lean boneless top round steaks, cut into strips
1/4 C. teriyaki sauce
4 -6 flour tortillas

Directions

1. Get a mixing bowl: Stir in it the teriyaki sauce and beef strips. Cover it and refrigerate it overnight.
2. Get a serving bowl: Toss in it the coleslaw mix with parsley, vinegar, sesame oil, ginger, and a pinch of salt.
3. Place the salad aside until ready to serve.
4. Place a large skillet over medium heat. Heat in it 1 tbsp of vegetable oil.
5. Drain half of the beef strips and cook them in the hot oil for 4 to 6 min. Drain them and place them aside.
6. Repeat the process with the remaining oil and beef.
7. Place a tortilla on a serving plate. Top it with some coleslaw mixture and beef strips.
8. Roll it tightly then repeat the process with the remaining ingredients. Serve them immediately.
9. Enjoy.

Glazed Asparagus Salad

Prep Time: 10 mins
Total Time: 20 mins

Servings per Recipe: 4
Calories   154.7
Fat   10.4g
Cholesterol   0.0mg
Sodium   361.5mg
Carbohydrates   12.1g
Protein   6.1g

Ingredients

1 lb. asparagus spear, trimmed and cut into pieces
1/2 C. slivered almonds
1 tbsp olive oil
1/8 C. cider vinegar
1/8 C. teriyaki sauce
1 tbsp sugar
1/4 tsp ground ginger
1/8-1/4 tsp pepper
salt

Directions

1. Bring a large saucepan of water to a boil. Cook in it the asparagus for 7 min.
2. Drain it and plunge it in cold water. Drain it and pat it dry.
3. Get a mixing bowl: Whisk in it the remaining ingredients. Add the asparagus and toss them to coat.
4. Place your salad in the fridge for at least 2 h then serve it.
5. Enjoy.

KIKI'S
Honey Salmon

Prep Time: 15 mins
Total Time: 30 mins

Servings per Recipe: 4
Calories 222.8
Fat 5.8g
Cholesterol 87.5mg
Sodium 413.3mg
Carbohydrates 6.6g
Protein 34.1g

Ingredients

3 tbsps orange juice
2 tbsps low sodium soy sauce
1 tbsp rice vinegar
1 tbsp honey
2 tsps grated ginger

1 tsp minced garlic
4 (6 ounces) salmon fillets

Directions

1. Before you do anything, preheat the oven to 450 F.
2. Get a roasting dish. Mix in it the orange juice with garlic, honey, ginger, soy sauce, and vinegar.
3. Season the salmon fillets with some salt and pepper. Coat them with the teriyaki sauce.
4. Cook them in the oven for 16 min. Serve them warm.
5. Enjoy.

Tex Mex Teriyaki Steak

Prep Time: 20 mins
Total Time: 35 mins

Servings per Recipe: 3
Calories   424.2
Fat   22.0g
Cholesterol   102.8mg
Sodium   2861.4mg
Carbohydrates   17.5g
Protein   37.5g

Ingredients

- 2 tbsps canola oil
- 1/2 tsp minced ginger
- 1/2 C. broccoli floret
- 1/2 C. carrot, slices
- 1/2 C. green beans, cut
- 1/2 C. red onion, sliced
- 3/4 C. teriyaki sauce
- 1 lb. beef sirloin flank steak, sliced

Directions

1. Place a large pan over high heat. Heat in it the oil.
2. Cook in it the veggies with ginger for 6 min. Stir in the beef and cook them for 4 min.
3. Add the teriyaki sauce and let them cook until the veggies become soft.
4. Serve your stir fry hot with some rice.
5. Enjoy.

5-INGREDIENT
Teriyaki Sauce

Prep Time: 15 mins
Total Time: 20 mins

Servings per Recipe: 4
Calories   243.2
Fat   0.1g
Cholesterol   0.0mg
Sodium   4024.0mg
Carbohydrates   55.4g
Protein   7.8g

Ingredients

1 C. soy sauce
1 C. sugar
1 tsp grated ginger
1 large garlic clove, minced
3 scallions, chopped

Directions

1. Place a heavy saucepan over medium heat. Stir in it the soy sauce with sugar until it dissolves.
2. Turn off the heat and the rest of the ingredients. Mix them well.
3. Spoon the sauce to a sterilized jar and seal it. Place it in the fridge until ready to use.
4. Enjoy.

Hibachi Tofu

🥣 Prep Time: 10 mins
🕐 Total Time: 20 mins

Servings per Recipe: 2
Calories   236.2
Fat   13.4g
Cholesterol   0.0mg
Sodium   826.1mg
Carbohydrates   14.9g
Protein   18.7g

Ingredients

- 15 ounces extra firm tofu, drained and sliced
- 3 tbsps low sodium soy sauce
- 1 tbsp rice vinegar
- 2 tsps sesame oil
- 1 tbsp honey
- 1 tsp ground ginger
- cooking spray

Directions

1. Place the tofu slices on a baking tray and cover them with another heavy tray.
2. Let them sit for 40. Drain the tofu slices and pat them dry.
3. Get a mixing bowl: Whisk in it the Tamari, rice vinegar, sesame oil, honey, ground ginger, a pinch of salt, and pepper.
4. Stir in the tofu slices and toss them to coat. Cover the bowl and let it sit for 2 h to overnight.
5. Place a large skillet over medium heat. Coat it with a cooking spray.
6. Drain the tofu slices and cook them for 2 to 3 min on each until they become golden brown.
7. Serve your tofu warm with some rice and roasted veggies.
8. Enjoy..

EVERYTHING
Teriyaki Dinner (Teriyaki Chicken and Teriyaki Rice)

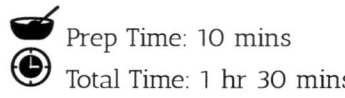

Prep Time: 10 mins
Total Time: 1 hr 30 mins

Servings per Recipe: 4
Calories	659.9
Fat	30.8g
Cholesterol	72.6mg
Sodium	3312.8mg
Carbohydrates	64.0g
Protein	32.4g

Ingredients

- 1 C. teriyaki sauce
- 3/4 C. pineapple juice
- 1/2 C. brown sugar
- 1/2 C. vinegar
- 1 tsp garlic powder
- 1/4 C. Worcestershire sauce
- 1/2 C. Italian salad dressing
- 1 - 1 1/2 lb. boneless chicken breast
- cooked rice
- 1 (4 ounces) cans crushed pineapple
- 3/4 C. cashew pieces
- various cooked vegetables, your choice

Directions

1. Place a heavy saucepan over medium heat.
2. Stir in it the teriyaki sauce with pineapple juice, brown sugar, vinegar, garlic powder, Worcestershire sauce, and Italian salad dressing. Cook them until they start boiling. Turn off the heat and let the sauce cool down completely.
3. Get a roasting dish: Place in it the chicken breasts and pour over them half of the marinade. Let them sit for 1 h in the fridge.
4. Before you do anything else, preheat the grill and grease it.
5. Drain the chicken breasts and grill them for 6 to 8 min on each side.
6. Prepare the rice by following the instructions on the package.
7. Get a mixing bowl: Stir in it the rice with pineapple, cashews, and a pinch of salt. Serve your pineapple rice with grilled chicken warm.
8. Enjoy.

Sticky Ginger Meatballs

Prep Time: 10 mins
Total Time: 35 mins

Servings per Recipe: 6
Calories   174.8
Fat   11.3g
Cholesterol   51.4mg
Sodium   510.6mg
Carbohydrates   2.2g
Protein   14.8g

Ingredients

- 1 lb. ground beef
- 1/4 C. teriyaki sauce
- 2 green onions, chopped
- 1/2 tsp grated gingerroot
- garlic salt

Directions

1. Before you do anything, preheat the oven to 350 F.
2. Get a mixing bowl: Mix in it the beef with teriyaki sauce, onion, ginger and a pinch of garlic salt.
3. Shape the mixture into bite size meatballs. Arrange them on a baking tray.
4. Let them cook for 25 to 32 min in the oven. Serve them warm.
5. Enjoy.

TERIYAKI
Bean Pods

Prep Time: 5 mins
Total Time: 11 mins

Servings per Recipe: 3
Calories 377.6
Fat 20.9g
Cholesterol 0.0mg
Sodium 946.2mg
Carbohydrates 30.3g
Protein 21.7g

Ingredients

1/4 C. teriyaki sauce
2 tbsps sesame oil
2 tbsps rice vinegar
2 tbsps dark brown sugar
1/4 C. water
16 ounces frozen edamame, in the pod
1 tbsp sesame seeds

Directions

1. Get a mixing bowl: Whisk in it the teriyaki sauce, sesame oil, rice vinegar and dark brown sugar.
2. Place a large pan over medium heat. Heat in it the water until it starts boiling.
3. Stir in the edamame and let it cook for 4 min.
4. Stir in the sauce mixture. Cook them until they start boiling.
5. Put on the lid and let them cook until the sauce becomes thick.
6. Stir in the sesame seeds and serve your salad warm with some rice.
7. Enjoy.

Kyoto Fish Kabobs

🥣 Prep Time: 20 mins
🕐 Total Time: 24 mins

Servings per Recipe: 1
Calories   24.0
Fat   0.6g
Cholesterol   8.3mg
Sodium   187.4mg
Carbohydrates   0.9g
Protein   3.5g

Ingredients

- 3 tbsps soy sauce
- 2 tbsps hoisin sauce
- 2 tsps rice vinegar
- 1 garlic clove, minced
- 1 salmon fillet, skinless
- 1 green onion, chopped
- toasted sesame seeds

Directions

1. Get a mixing bowl: Whisk in it the soy and hoisin sauces, vinegar and garlic.
2. Cut the salmon fillet into strips and add them to the bowl. Toss them to coat. Let them sit for 20 min.
3. Before you do anything, preheat the grill and grease it.
4. Drain the fish strips and thread them onto skewers. Grill them for 2 to 4 min on each side.
5. Serve them warm. Garnish them with green onion and sesame seeds.
6. Enjoy.

MY FIRST
Teriyaki Sauce

Prep Time: 20 mins
Total Time: 20 mins

Servings per Recipe: 1
Calories	665.1
Fat	0.1g
Cholesterol	0.0mg
Sodium	11097.8mg
Carbohydrates	151.2g
Protein	16.0g

Ingredients

- 1/2 C. Japanese soya (soy) sauce
- 1/2 C. rice vinegar
- 1/2 C. sugar
- 1 pinch ginger
- 2 tbsps honey
- 1 tsp salt
- 1 minced garlic clove

Directions

1. Place a large saucepan over medium heat.
2. Stir in it all the ingredients. Cook them until they start boiling.
3. Lower the heat and let the sauce cook for 14 to 16 min until it becomes thick.
4. Turn off the heat and let the sauce cool down completely.
5. Spoon into a glass jar and store it in the fridge until ready to use.
6. Enjoy.

Japanese House Quinoa

Prep Time: 25 mins
Total Time: 25 mins

Servings per Recipe: 4
Calories   205.4
Fat   6.0g
Cholesterol   0.0mg
Sodium   887.0mg
Carbohydrates   30.2g
Protein   8.3g

Ingredients

- 1 C. dry quinoa, rinsed and drained
- 2 C. water
- 4 garlic cloves, minced
- 1 tsp ginger, grated
- 3 1/2 tbsps tamari
- 2 1/2 tbsps agave nectar
- 2 tsps lemon juice
- 2 tsps sesame oil
- 1 tbsp sesame seeds
- 3 tbsps green onions, sliced

Directions

1. Place a large saucepan over medium heat. Stir in it the garlic with quinoa and water.
2. Season them with a pinch of salt. Cook them until they start boiling.
3. Lower the heat and put on the lid. Let them cook for 14 min until the quinoa is done.
4. Get a large mixing bowl: Whisk in it the ginger, tamari, agave nectar, lemon juice and sesame oil.
5. Add the quinoa and mix them with a fork. Place it aside to rest for 6 min.
6. Garnish your quinoa salad with sesame seeds and green onion then serve it.
7. Enjoy.

60-MINUTE
Japanese Pilaf

Prep Time: 30 mins
Total Time: 50 mins

Servings per Recipe: 1
Calories   517.7
Fat   6.7g
Cholesterol   68.4mg
Sodium   1096.6mg
Carbohydrates   62.6g
Protein   37.1g

Ingredients

1 boneless skinless chicken breast, diced
1 tsp gingerroot, diced
1 garlic clove, smashed and diced
1 tbsp soy sauce
1 tbsp apple cider vinegar
1 tsp sugar
1 (4 ounces) cans mushrooms, sliced

1/3 C. raw rice
1 tsp cooking oil
chicken stock

Directions

1. Get a roasting dish: Toss in it the chicken with ginger, garlic, soy sauce, apple cider vinegar, sugar, a pinch of salt and pepper.
2. Drain the mushrooms and reserve their liquid.
3. Place a large pan over medium heat. Heat in it the oil. Brown in it the chicken dices for 4 min.
4. Stir in the rice with mushroom, a pinch of salt and pepper.
5. Add enough water to the mushroom liquid to complete 2/3 C.. Stir it into the skillet.
6. Put on the lid and lower the heat. Let them cook for 16 min.
7. Remove the hit and cook the pilaf for an extra 6 min. Serve it warm.
8. Enjoy.

Big World Burgers

 Prep Time: 10 mins
 Total Time: 20 mins

Servings per Recipe: 4
Calories 492.6
Fat 28.1g
Cholesterol 106.5mg
Sodium 1144.6mg
Carbohydrates 24.4g
Protein 33.2g

Ingredients

- 1 lb. ground beef
- 1/4 C. teriyaki marinade
- 1 (3 ounce) cans French-fried onions
- 4 slices cheddar cheese
- 4 hamburger buns, split

Directions

1. Before you do anything, preheat the grill and grease it.
2. Get a large mixing bowl: Combine in it the beef with teriyaki marinade, fried onion, a pinch of salt, and pepper.
3. Mix them. Shape the mixture into 4 burgers.
4. Place them on the grill and cook them for 5 to 6 min on each side.
5. Assemble your burgers with cheese then serve them immediately.
6. Enjoy.

TERIYAKI
Orzo

🥣 Prep Time: 15 mins
🕐 Total Time: 25 mins

Servings per Recipe: 4
Calories   849.7 C
Fat   31.3g
Cholesterol   153.6mg
Sodium   3001.4mg
Carbohydrates   55.8g
Protein   81.8g

Ingredients

4 salmon fillets
1-ounce canola oil
1-ounce soy sauce
8 ounces teriyaki sauce
8 ounces orzo pasta, precooked
2 garlic cloves, minced
2 tbsps olive oil, combined with garlic

1/2 C. red bell pepper, diced
1/3 C. parmesan cheese
8 ounces spinach, julienned

Directions

1. Before you do anything, preheat the grill and grease it.
2. Coat the salmon fillets with soy sauce then grill them for 3 min on each side.
3. Brush the salmon fillets with teriyaki sauce then grill them for 2 to 3 min on each side.
4. Prepare the orzo by following the instructions on the package.
5. Place a large skillet over medium heat. Heat in it the oil.
6. Cook in it the garlic with bell pepper and cooked orzo for 2 min.
7. Stir in the parmesan cheese. Turn off the heat and fold the spinach into the mixture.
8. Serve your bell orzo warm with grilled salmon.
9. Enjoy.

Tilapia Japan

🍳 Prep Time: 5 mins
⏱ Total Time: 15 mins

Servings per Recipe: 5
Calories   245.6
Fat   4.8g
Cholesterol   62.5mg
Sodium   1680.0mg
Carbohydrates   23.3g
Protein   28.1g

Ingredients

- 1 tbsp oil
- 5 tilapia fillets
- 1/2 C. brown sugar
- 1/4 C. seasoned rice vinegar
- 1/2 C. soy sauce
- 1 tsp ginger, grated
- 1/2 tsp garlic, minced

Directions

1. Season the tilapia fillets with some salt and pepper.
2. Place a large skillet over medium heat. Heat in it the oil.
3. Cook in it the tilapia fillets for 3 to 5 min on each side.
4. Get a mixing bowl: Whisk in it the soy sauce with brown sugar, vinegar, ginger, garlic, and a pinch of salt.
5. Pour the sauce over the fish fillets. Let them cook until the sauce becomes thick.
6. Serve them hot with some steamed rice.
7. Enjoy.

TERIYAKI
Stir Fried Veggies

Prep Time: 10 mins
Total Time: 20 mins

Servings per Recipe: 6
Calories 60.9
Fat 2.3g
Cholesterol 5.0mg
Sodium 377.3mg
Carbohydrates 9.3g
Protein 2.2g

Ingredients

1 lb. green beans, cut into pieces
2 medium carrots, cut into strips
1 tbsp butter
1 tsp cornstarch
3 tbsps teriyaki sauce

1 tbsp water
1 tsp sesame seeds

Directions

1. Place a saucepan of water over high heat. Cook in it the green beans and carrots for 9 min.
2. Drain them and pat them dry.
3. Place a large skillet over medium heat. Heat in it the butter until it melts.
4. Add the cornstarch with water and teriyaki sauce. Mix them well.
5. Stir in the veggies and cook them for 1 min.
6. Serve your veggies stir fry hot with some sesame seeds.
7. Enjoy.

Orange Fish

Prep Time: 45 mins
Total Time: 55 mins

Servings per Recipe: 4
Calories   491.8
Fat   14.0g
Cholesterol   146.2mg
Sodium   745.1mg
Carbohydrates   21.4g
Protein   66.4g

Ingredients

- 1/3 C. maple syrup, real
- 1/3 C. orange juice
- 2 tbsps soy sauce
- 1/4 C. onion, chopped
- 1 garlic clove, minced
- 4 salmon fillets

Directions

1. Get a large zip lock bag: Place in it all the ingredients. Seal it and shake them to coat.
2. Place it in the fridge for 1 h.
3. Before you do anything, preheat the oven to 375 F.
4. Drain the salmon fillets from the marinade and arrange them on a baking tray.
5. Bake them for 11 min. Serve them warm.
6. Enjoy.

SIMPLE
Ginger Teriyaki Salad

Prep Time: 10 mins
Total Time: 25 mins

Servings per Recipe: 2
Calories	172.9
Fat	7.6g
Cholesterol	0.0mg
Sodium	1017.9mg
Carbohydrates	21.7g
Protein	9.0g

Ingredients

- 2 (8 ounces) packages mushrooms
- 2 tbsps sugar
- 2 tbsps soy sauce
- 1 tbsp white vinegar
- 1 tbsp cooking oil
- 1/4-1/2 tsp red pepper
- 1/4-1/2 tsp ground ginger
- 1/8-1/4 tsp garlic powder
- 2 tbsps green onions, sliced

Directions

1. Place a heavy saucepan over medium heat.
2. Stir in it the sugar, soy sauce, vinegar, oil, red pepper, ginger and garlic powder.
3. Cook them for 1 min. Stir in the onion with mushrooms. Cook them for 3 min.
4. Serve your salad warm with some rice.
5. Enjoy.

Teriyaki Rice Cakes

Prep Time: 30 mins
Total Time: 40 mins

Servings per Recipe: 8
Calories   272.9
Fat   2.6g
Cholesterol   0.0mg
Sodium   970.2mg
Carbohydrates   55.8g
Protein   5.3g

Ingredients

- 5 C. water
- 1 tsp salt
- 2 1/2 C. long-grain white rice
- 1/3 C. soy sauce
- 1/3 C. packed brown sugar
- 1 tsp toasted sesame oil
- 1 tbsp peanut oil

Directions

1. Place a large saucepan over high heat. Heat in it the water with salt until it starts boiling. Stir in the rice and bring it to another boil. Put on the lid and lower the heat.
2. Let the rice cook for 26 min. Once the time is up, turn off the heat and let it sit for 12 min.
3. Cover the bottom of a cake pan with a piece of plastic wrap. Spoon into it the rice in an even layer.
4. Lay over it a piece of plastic wrap and pat it down. Place it aside until it cools down completely.
5. Place it in the fridge overnight.
6. Discard the top wrap and flip the rice cake to a serving plate then discard the bottom wrap.
7. Slice the rice cake into 8 pieces.
8. Get a mixing bowl: Whisk in it the soy sauce with brown sugar, sesame, and peanut oil to make the teriyaki sauce.
9. Before you do anything, preheat the grill and grease it.
10. Coat the rice slices with the teriyaki sauce. Cook them over the grill for 2 to 4 min on each side.
11. Serve them warm.
12. Enjoy.

SUMMER
Teriyaki BBQ

Prep Time: 15 mins
Total Time: 40 mins

Servings per Recipe: 2
Calories　　　　264.1
Fat　　　　　　2.2g
Cholesterol　　 68.4mg
Sodium　　　　1475.6mg
Carbohydrates　27.5g
Protein　　　　36.1g

Ingredients

2 boneless skinless chicken breast halves
1 small zucchini, cut into bite-size pieces
1 large green pepper, cut into chunks
2 small onions, quartered, each quarter cut in half
8 ounces mushrooms, halved
10 cloves garlic
1/4-1/2 C. teriyaki marinade
salt and pepper
garlic powder
5-6 Bbq skewers

Directions

1. Thread the veggies onto skewers while alternating between them.
2. Make 5 slits in each chicken breast. Press a clove of garlic into each slit.
3. Season them with some garlic powder, salt and pepper then coat them with the teriyaki sauce.
4. Before you do anything, preheat the grill and grease its grates with oil.
5. Arrange over it the chicken breasts and veggies skewers.
6. Cook them for 5 to 8 min on each side until they are done.
7. Serve your grill chicken and veggies warm.
8. Enjoy.

Teriyaki Slaw

Prep Time: 20 mins
Total Time: 35 mins

Servings per Recipe: 4
Calories   113.0
Fat   3.8g
Cholesterol   0.0mg
Sodium   70.0mg
Carbohydrates   18.8g
Protein   3.9g

Ingredients

1 medium head of cabbage, shredded
2 large carrots, peeled and sliced
1 medium zucchini, sliced
3 garlic cloves, minced
1 - 2 tbsp extra-virgin olive oil
2 tbsps low-sodium teriyaki sauce
black pepper

Directions

1. Place a large pan over medium heat. Heat in it the oil.
2. Cook in it the carrots for 2 min. Stir in the cabbage and cook them for 3 min.
3. Stir in the zucchini and cook them for another 2 min.
4. Stir in the teriyaki sauce with a pinch of salt and pepper. Cook them for 8 min.
5. Serve your teriyaki slaw warm.
6. Enjoy.

TERIYAKI
Pasta Salad

Prep Time: 20 mins
Total Time: 37 mins

Servings per Recipe: 2
Calories   636.9
Fat   20.1g
Cholesterol   115.2mg
Sodium   3575.6mg
Carbohydrates   59.8g
Protein   54.7g

Ingredients

3.5 oz. dried somen noodles, or any thin noodle
4 tbsps soy sauce
3 tbsps rice vinegar
2 tsps brown sugar
1/4 C. water
2 tbsps canola oil
2 tsps cornflour

12.5 oz. skinless chicken breasts, cut into bite-sized pieces
1 carrot, julienned
1 bunch bok choy, chopped
1 spring onion
2 tsps grated gingerroot

Directions

1. Get a mixing bowl: Whisk in it 2 tsp of water with cornflour.
2. Bring a large pot of water to a boil. Cook in it the noodles for 4 min.
3. Drain it and place it aside.
4. Get a mixing bowl: Whisk in it the soy sauce, rice vinegar, brown sugar, and water to make the teriyaki sauce.
5. Place a large skillet over high heat. Heat in it 1 tbsp of oil.
6. Cook in it the chicken for 6 min. Season it with a pinch of salt and pepper. Drain it and place it aside.
7. Heat the rest of the oil in the skillet. Cook in it the carrot with bok choy for 8 min. Stir in the somen noodles and cook them for 40 sec.
8. Stir in the cooked chicken with green onion, ginger, a pinch of salt and pepper.
9. Add the cornstarch mixture with teriyaki sauce. Cook them while stirring until the sauce becomes thick.
10. Add the pasta and toss them to coat. Serve your salad warm.
11. Enjoy.

Homemade Teriyaki Chips

Prep Time: 5 mins
Total Time: 20 mins

Servings per Recipe: 6
Calories   688.4
Fat   7.7g
Cholesterol   19.2mg
Sodium   1450.6mg
Carbohydrates   130.6g
Protein   21.3g

Ingredients

Teriyaki
20 - 22 egg roll wraps
2 tbsps teriyaki sauce
2 tbsps honey
1 tbsp vegetable oil
Chips
20 - 22 egg roll wraps

1/2 tsp Thai red curry paste
2 tbsps lime juice
1 tbsp vegetable oil

Directions

1. To prepare the teriyaki chips:
2. Before you do anything, preheat the oven to 400 F.
3. Cover a baking sheet with a parchment paper. Place it aside.
4. Get a mixing bowl: Mix in it the teriyaki sauce, honey and peanut oil. Slice each egg roll into 3 triangles. Coat them with the teriyaki sauce and lay them on the lined up sheet.
5. Cook them in the oven for 16 min until they become golden and crunchy.
6. To prepare the spicy chips:
7. Cover a baking sheet with a parchment paper. Place it aside.
8. Get a mixing bowl: Mix in it the Thai curry paste, lime juice, and oil.
9. Slice each egg roll into 3 triangles. Coat them with the curry mixture and lay them on the lined up sheet.
10. Cook them in the oven for 16 min as well until they become golden and crunchy. Serve your chips with your favorite dip. Enjoy.

BELLA
Burger Teriyaki

Prep Time: 10 mins
Total Time: 18 mins

Servings per Recipe: 4
Calories 455.1
Fat 19.7g
Cholesterol 31.0mg
Sodium 1510.4mg
Carbohydrates 52.5g
Protein 19.2g

Ingredients

- 4 large portabella mushrooms, stemmed
- 2 ounces ginger, peeled and crushed
- 1 garlic clove, peeled and crushed
- 1/4 C. soy sauce
- 3 tsps artificial sweetener
- 1 tbsp canola oil
- 4 kaiser rolls
- 1/4 C. light mayonnaise
- 1 sweet onion, sliced
- 4 lettuce leaves
- 1 large tomatoes, sliced
- 4 slices swiss cheese

Directions

1. Get a large zip lock bag; combine in it the garlic with ginger, soy sauce, sweetener, and oil.
2. Season the mushrooms with some salt and pepper. Add them to the bag and seal it.
3. Shake them to coat. Place it aside for 20 min.
4. Place a large pan over high heat. Add the mushrooms to the hot pan and cook them for 3 min on each side until the sauce evaporates.
5. Coat the bottom of the kaiser rolls with mayo.
6. Top them with a lettuce leaf followed by hot mushroom, cheese, tomato slice and top bun.
7. Serve your sandwiches immediately.
8. Enjoy.

Sticky Chicken

Prep Time: 20 mins
Total Time: 45 mins

Servings per Recipe: 4
Calories   451.9
Fat   8.0g
Cholesterol   0.0mg
Sodium   7041.2mg
Carbohydrates   86.7g
Protein   14.0g

Ingredients

6 bone in chicken pieces
1 3/4 C. soy sauce
1 tsp grated lime peel
1/2 C. lime juice
3 garlic cloves, peeled and flattened with a knife
2 scallions, sliced green and white parts separated
3 inches ginger, peeled and sliced
2 tbsps honey
1 1/3 C. sugar
2 tbsps sesame oil
1 tbsp sesame seeds

Directions

1. Place a heavy saucepan over medium heat: Stir in it the soy sauce, lime peel, lime juice, garlic, scallion whites, ginger and honey until they honey melts. Get a roasting dish: Place in it the chicken pieces and pour over them half of the honey mixture.
2. Put on the lid and let them sit for 60 min in the fridge.
3. Stir the rest of the sugar into the remaining marinade. Bring it to a boil. Lower the heat and let it cook for 12 until it becomes heavy to make the glaze.
4. Place it aside to cool down for a while.
5. Before you do anything, preheat the grill and grease it.
6. Lay a piece of foil over the grill and poke it several times to create holes. Drain the chicken pieces and coat them with the sesame oil. Grill them for 6 to 7 min on each side.
7. Coat the chicken pieces with some of the glaze and grill them for another 6 to 7 min on each side.
8. Serve your chicken hot with the remaining glaze and rice.
9. Enjoy.

EGG NOODLE
Teriyaki

Prep Time: 10 mins
Total Time: 15 mins

Servings per Recipe: 4
Calories 1010.7
Fat 32.3g
Cholesterol 230.2mg
Sodium 1272.3mg
Carbohydrates 94.0g
Protein 83.2g

Ingredients

4 tbsps maple syrup
4 salmon fillets, skinned and cut into bit size pieces
2 spring onions, green onion sliced
1 red capsicum, deseeded and sliced
7 oz. snow peas
1 tbsp sesame oil
1 lime, juice
14 oz egg noodles, cooked

Directions

1. Place a large deep skillet over high heat. Heat in it the oil.
2. Cook in it the ginger with garlic for 40 sec. Stir in the maple syrup with soy sauce.
3. Cook them for 1 min. Stir in the salmon and cook them for 3 min.
4. Fold the spring onions with capsicum, snow peas, a pinch of salt and pepper. Cook them for 3 min.
5. Stir in the lime juice with sesame oil. Turn off the heat.
6. Fold the egg noodles into the mixture and serve it hot.
7. Enjoy.

Full Mango Skillet

Prep Time: 15 mins
Total Time: 30 mins

Servings per Recipe: 4
Calories 474.4
Fat 27.7g
Cholesterol 98.8mg
Sodium 919.0mg
Carbohydrates 32.1g
Protein 26.8g

Ingredients

8 ounces sliced fresh mushrooms
1 medium red onion, chopped
3 tbsps butter
1 lb. boneless beef top sirloin steak, trimmed and sliced
16 ounces mangoes, pitted and cut into chunks
1/2 C. beef stock
1 tbsp cornstarch
1/4 C. teriyaki sauce
ground black pepper
1/4 lb. snow peas
4 green onions, chopped
1 - 2 C. steamed cooked brown rice

Directions

1. Place a large pan over medium heat. Heat in it the butter.
2. Cook in it the onion with mushrooms for 4 min. Stir in the beef and cook them for 3 min.
3. Stir in the stock and let them cook for 6 min.
4. Get a mixing bowl: Mix in it the teriyaki sauce with cornstarch. Add them to the pan with a pinch of salt and pepper.
5. Cook them until the sauce becomes thick. Add the mango with green onions and snow peas.
6. Serve your fruity stir fry with white rice.
7. Enjoy.

WILD RICE
Teriyaki

🍳 Prep Time: 1 hr
🕐 Total Time: 1 hr

Servings per Recipe: 8
Calories   131.6
Fat   4.9g
Cholesterol   7.7mg
Sodium   553.4mg
Carbohydrates   18.5g
Protein   4.1g

Ingredients

1 C. wild rice
2 C. water
2 beef bouillon cubes
1 tbsp butter
1 small onion, chopped
1/2 C. celery, chopped
1/2 C. carrot, shredded

1 tbsp butter
1 tbsp olive oil
1 garlic clove, pressed
1 C. sliced mushrooms
3 tbsps Kikkoman teriyaki sauce

Directions

1. Place a large saucepan over high heat. Stir in it the rice with 2 C. of water, 2 bouillon cubes, and butter.
2. Cook them until they start boiling. Lower the heat and put on the lid.
3. Let them cook for 46 min. Turn off the heat and let it sit for 12 min.
4. Once the time is up, stir it with a fork and place it aside.
5. Place a large skillet over medium heat. Heat in it the oil.
6. Cook in it the onion with celery and carrot for 6 min.
7. Stir in the mushroom with garlic, a pinch of salt and pepper. Cook them for 5 min.
8. Stir in the teriyaki sauce and cook them for 3 min. Add the rice and toss them to coat.
9. Serve your stir fried rice and veggies warm.
10. Enjoy.

Teriyaki Seafood Skewers

Prep Time: 20 mins
Total Time: 30 mins

Servings per Recipe: 4
Calories   182.1
Fat   4.6g
Cholesterol   62.3mg
Sodium   677.3mg
Carbohydrates   16.9g
Protein   18.8g

Ingredients

Teriyaki
1/4 C. low sodium soy sauce
3 tbsps dark brown sugar
1 1/2 tbsps rice vinegar
1 tbsp minced peeled fresh ginger
1/4 tsp crushed red pepper flakes
1 garlic clove, minced
Cornstarch Mix
1 1/2 tsps cornstarch
1 1/2 tsps water

Skewers
16 large shrimp, peeled and deveined
16 sea scallops
16 mushrooms, halved
green onion
1 tbsp vegetable oil
cooking spray
8 wooden 12-inch skewers

Directions

1. To prepare the glaze:
2. Place a heavy saucepan over high heat. Whisk in it all the glaze ingredients. Cook them until they start boiling. Let it cook for 2 to 3 min. Get a mixing bowl: Whisk in it the water with cornstarch. Add it to the glaze sauce and mix them. Cook them until they start boiling again. Let them cook for 2 min. Place it aside to cool down.
3. Before you do anything, preheat the grill and grease it.
4. Press 2 scallops onto a metal skewer followed by 2 shrimps, 4 mushroom halves, and 3 green onion pieces.
5. Repeat the process with the remaining ingredients. Coat them with oil and grill them for 1 to 2 min on each side.
6. Coat them with some glaze and grill them for 2 to 3 min on each side. Serve your kabobs warm with the remaining glaze. Enjoy.

TERIYAKI
Pasta

Prep Time: 45 mins
Total Time: 1 hr 45 mins

Servings per Recipe: 12
Calories 286.1
Fat 5.8g
Cholesterol 21.9mg
Sodium 706.2mg
Carbohydrates 42.6g
Protein 15.7g

Ingredients

1 lb. boneless skinless chicken breast, cut into bite size pieces
1/2 C. soy sauce
1/2 C. sugar
1 tsp minced garlic
1 tsp minced ginger
1 1/2 tsps rice vinegar
4 tbsps canola oil
1 lb. linguine

1 large onion, sliced into strips
1 bell pepper, sliced into strips
2 carrots, sliced into strips
1 (6 ounces) cans sliced water chestnuts
1 (6 ounces) cans sliced bamboo shoots

Directions

1. Get a zip lock bag: Pour in it the soy sauce, sugar, garlic, ginger, vinegar, and 2 tbsp oil. Add the chicken dices and seal the bag. Shake it to coat. Place it overnight in the fridge.
2. Place a large skillet over medium heat. Heat in it the oil.
3. Drain the chicken pieces and cook them for 7 min. Season them with a pinch of salt and pepper.
4. Place the chicken marinade aside for later use.
5. Drain it and place it aside. Cook the carrot in the same pan for 2 min. Stir in the onion with pepper, chestnuts, bamboo shoots, a pinch of salt and pepper. cook them for 4 min.
6. Stir in the cooked chicken with reserved marinade. Bring them to a boil and cook them for 6 min.
7. Add the pasta and toss them to coat. Serve your pasta and chicken stir fry immediately.
8. Enjoy.

Teriyaki Cod

🥣 Prep Time: 5 mins
🕐 Total Time: 30 mins

Servings per Recipe: 2
Calories   102.1
Fat   3.8g
Cholesterol   10.0mg
Sodium   2793.7mg
Carbohydrates   12.2g
Protein   4.5g

Ingredients

- 2 black cod steaks
- 2 tsps melted butter
- 1/2 C. teriyaki marinade
- 2 cloves garlic, minced
- black pepper

Directions

1. Get a zip lock bag. Combine in it the melted butter, marinade, garlic, and a few dashes of pepper.
2. Add the cod steaks and seal the bag. Shake it to coat. place it aside for 25 min.
3. Before you do anything, preheat the grill and grease it.
4. Drain the cod steaks and grill them for 9 to 12 min on each side while basting them with the marinade.
5. Serve your cod steaks warm.
6. Enjoy.

VEGETARIAN
Teriyaki Skillet

Prep Time: 10 mins
Total Time: 25 mins

Servings per Recipe: 4
Calories 179.7
Fat 14.4g
Cholesterol 0.0mg
Sodium 706.6mg
Carbohydrates 5.4g
Protein 9.7g

Ingredients

14 ounces extra firm tofu, drained and diced
3 tbsps sesame seed oil

1 C. broccoli floret
1/4 C. teriyaki sauce

Directions

1. Place a large pan over high heat. Heat in it the oil.
2. Cook in it the tofu for 3 to 4 min. Stir in the broccoli and cook them for 11 mi.
3. Stir in the teriyaki sauce with a pinch of salt and pepper.
4. Lower the heat and let them cook until the sauce thickens.
5. Serve it hot with some rice.
6. Enjoy.

Teriyaki Backyard Burgers

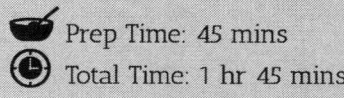

Prep Time: 45 mins
Total Time: 1 hr 45 mins

Servings per Recipe: 1
Calories 1178.0
Fat 39.0g
Cholesterol 135.9mg
Sodium 22667.5mg
Carbohydrates 127.6g
Protein 74.3g

Ingredients

- 1/3 lb. hamburger meat
- 1 hamburger bun with sesame seeds
- 1 tbsp mayonnaise
- 1/4 C. shredded lettuce
- 1 pineapple ring
- 2 C. teriyaki sauce
- 2 slices tomatoes
- 1 slice cheddar cheese

Directions

1. Shape the burger meat into a patty. Place it in a shallow bowl and cover it with 1 C. of teriyaki sauce.
2. Place the pineapple ring in a shallow bowl. Cover it with 1 C. of teriyaki sauce.
3. Let them sit for 35 min.
4. Before you do anything, preheat the grill and grease it.
5. Grill the burger patty for 4 to 6 min on each side. Lay over it the cheese slice and let it sit for 1 min.
6. Place the pineapple ring on the grill and grill it for 1 min on each side.
7. Coat the inside of the burger bun with mayo.
8. Arrange the tomato slices over the bottom half followed by burger patty, pineapple ring, and lettuce.
9. Serve your burger immediately.
10. Enjoy.

SUSHI
Chisaka

Prep Time: 1 hr
Total Time: 1 hr 30 mins

Servings per Recipe: 1
Calories   164.9
Fat   2.1g
Cholesterol   0.0mg
Sodium   111.2mg
Carbohydrates   33.1g
Protein   2.7g

Ingredients

- 9 oz. eggplants
- 4 tbsps low sodium soy sauce
- 4 tbsps maple syrup
- 1 tbsp ginger, grated
- 1 tsp garlic, grated
- 2 tbsps sesame oil
- 1/2 tsp ground black pepper
- 3 C. water
- 4 tbsp rice vinegar
- 2 tbsps maple syrup
- 1/2 tbsp sesame oil
- 6 sheets nori, Japanese
- 1 tbsp sesame seeds, toasted

Directions

1. Get a mixing bowl: Whisk in it the soy sauce, maple syrup, ginger, garlic, sesame oil, and pepper.
2. Slice the eggplant into 3 thick slices then use a fork to pierce them several times.
3. Place them in the soy sauce mixture and let them sit for 20 min. Place a soup pot over medium heat. Stir in the water with rice and a pinch of salt.
4. Cook them until they start boiling. Lower the heat and put on the lid. Let them cook for 22 min. Before you do anything else, preheat the grill and grease it.
5. Cook over it the eggplant slices for 3 to 4 min on each side until they become charred. Cut them into thin strips.
6. Get a mixing bowl: Whisk in it the rice vinegar, maple syrup, sesame oil, and sesame seeds.
7. Drizzle the dressing over the rice and mix it with a fork.
8. Place a nori sheet over a bamboo mat. Spread over the rice in an even layer. Arrange over them the eggplant strips then roll it gently and firmly.
9. Slice the sushi into 8 pieces. Serve it with a sauce of your choice. Enjoy.

How to Make Teriyaki Sauce

Prep Time: 6 mins
Total Time: 12 mins

Servings per Recipe: 15
Calories   25.5
Fat   0.0g
Cholesterol   0.0mg
Sodium   269.9mg
Carbohydrates   6.0g
Protein   0.5g

Ingredients

1/4 C. soy sauce
1/4 tsp garlic powder
1/2 tsp ground ginger
1 C. water
2 tbsps brown sugar
1 tbsp honey
1 - 2 drop stevia
1/4 C. cold water
2 tbsps cornstarch

Directions

1. Get a mixing bowl: Whisk in it the cornstarch with 1/4 C. of water.
2. Place a heavy saucepan over medium heat.
3. Stir in it the soy sauce with garlic powder, ginger, 1/4 C. of water, sugar, honey, and a pinch of salt.
4. Add the cornstarch mix and combine them well. Cook them until the sauce becomes thick.
5. Stir in it the stevia then serve it warm.
6. Enjoy.

ASIAN Fusion Chicken Wings

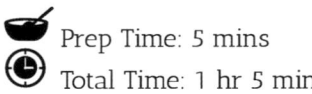

Prep Time: 5 mins
Total Time: 1 hr 5 mins

Servings per Recipe: 4
Calories   701.7
Fat   47.7g
Cholesterol   205.2mg
Sodium   4406.6mg
Carbohydrates   16.8g
Protein   48.1g

Ingredients

1/4 C. butter, melted
2 lbs. pre-cut chicken wings, cut in two
garlic salt
1 1/2 C. teriyaki sauce
blue cheese dressing
pepper

Directions

1. Before you do anything, preheat the oven to 400 F.
2. Sprinkle some garlic salt and pepper all over the chicken wings.
3. Pour the melted butter and Arrange over it the chicken wings.
4. Drizzle over them the teriyaki sauce and stir them to coat.
5. Place them in the oven and let them cook for 22 min.
6. Serve your chicken wings hot with some blue cheese dressing and rice.
7. Enjoy.

Teriyaki Spaghetti Squash

Prep Time: 5 mins
Total Time: 20 mins

Servings per Recipe: 4	
Calories	339.6
Fat	4.6g
Cholesterol	239.1mg
Sodium	2551.7mg
Carbohydrates	46.1g
Protein	32.5g

Ingredients

- 16 ounces cooked shrimp, peeled and deveined
- 1 (14 ounces) bags classic coleslaw mix
- 6 -8 uncooked scallions, chopped
- 8 tbsps teriyaki sauce
- 4 -5 lbs. spaghetti squash

Directions

1. Slice the squash in half and discard it seeds. Place it in a deep roasting dish and pour around it 1/4 C. of water.
2. Layover it a cling foil to cover it and microwave it for 7 min on high.
3. Discard the foil and microwave it for another 7 min on high.
4. Cover the squash halves again and let them rest for 6 min.
5. Place a pan over medium heat. Stir in it the slaw with teriyaki sauce, scallions, and a pinch of salt and pepper.
6. Cook them for 6 min. Stir in the shrimp and cook them for 5 min.
7. Shred the squash with a fork and add it to the pan. Divide it among 4 serving plates.
8. Spoon the stir-fried shrimp mixture over the spaghetti squash then serve them warm.
9. Enjoy.

WEST INDIAN
Teriyaki Fish

Prep Time: 15 mins
Total Time: 30 mins

Servings per Recipe: 2
Calories	365.6
Fat	15.5g
Cholesterol	51.6mg
Sodium	1866.5mg
Carbohydrates	31.4g
Protein	27.1g

Ingredients

- 2 tbsps prepared teriyaki sauce
- 2 tbsps dark soy sauce
- 2 1/2 tbsps brown sugar
- 1 1/2 tbsps olive oil
- 2 tbsps grated ginger
- 1 tbsp red vinegar
- 2 tbsps sliced scallions
- 1 1/2 small limes
- 1/2 tsp lime zest
- 1 pinch red pepper flakes
- 1/2 tsp chopped garlic
- 1 pinch salt
- 1 pinch black pepper
- 8 ounces salmon fillets

Directions

1. Get a mixing bowl: Whisk in it the Teriyaki sauce, soy sauce, brown sugar, grated ginger, red vinegar.
2. Stir in the scallions, lime zest, and juice of one lime, chopped garlic, oil, a pinch of salt and red pepper flakes.
3. Place a large skillet over medium heat. Pour in it the sauce and heat it for 2 min.
4. Sprinkle some salt and pepper over the salmon fillets.
5. Add them to the pan and let them cook for 3 to 4 min on each side and until the sauce becomes thick.
6. Serve your glazed salmon fillets hot with some rice.
7. Enjoy.

Teriyaki Burritos

Prep Time: 5 mins
Total Time: 20 mins

Servings per Recipe: 4
Calories   81.7
Fat   7.1g
Cholesterol   0.0mg
Sodium   2.9mg
Carbohydrates   4.6g
Protein   0.8g

Ingredients

- 2 tbsps canola oil
- 1 (14 ounce) packages mixed peppers, strips
- 1 1/2 lbs. chicken breast fillets, sliced
- 1/4 C. Teriyaki Sauce
- 8 small (6-inch) flour tortillas, warmed

Directions

1. Place a large pan over medium heat. Heat in it 1 tbsp of oil. Cook in it the peppers for 5 min.
2. Stir in the rest of the oil with chicken, a pinch of salt and pepper. Cook them for 3 min.
3. Stir in the teriyaki sauce and let them cook for 3 to 4 min until the chicken is done.
4. Spoon your fajita into tortillas then serve them warm.
5. Enjoy.

TERIYAKI
Beef

🥘 Prep Time: 20 mins
🕒 Total Time: 25 mins

Servings per Recipe: 4
Calories 307.3
Fat 12.5g
Cholesterol 85.0mg
Sodium 1459.4mg
Carbohydrates 13.1g
Protein 33.4g

Ingredients

1 1/4 lbs. boneless beef top sirloin steaks
1/2 C. teriyaki marinade, & sauce
2 tbsps sugar
2 tsps cornstarch

2 tbsps vegetable oil
hot cooked white rice
steamed vegetables

Directions

1. Slice the steaks into 1/4 inch strips.
2. Get a mixing bowl: Whisk in it the teriyaki sauce and sugar. Reserve 3 tbsp of the mixture aside.
3. Add the beef strips to the bowl and cover it. Let them sit for 20 min.
4. Get a mixing bowl: Whisk in it 2/3 C. of water with 3 tbsp of the reserved marinade, and cornstarch.
5. Place a large pan over medium heat. Heat in it the oil. Cook in it the beef strips for 3 min.
6. Stir in the cornstarch mixture with a pinch of salt and pepper. Let them cook for 2 min until the sauce becomes thick.
7. Spoon your teriyaki beef over the rice then serve it warm.
8. Enjoy.

Mediterranean Meets Japanese Skillet

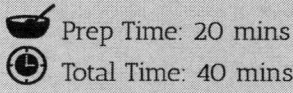 Prep Time: 20 mins
Total Time: 40 mins

Servings per Recipe: 4
Calories 719.0
Fat 56.0g
Cholesterol 148.0mg
Sodium 1360.1mg
Carbohydrates 15.0g
Protein 38.6g

Ingredients

- olive oil
- 2 lb. lamb fillets, sliced into strips
- 2 tsps sesame oil
- 2 garlic cloves, crushed
- 1 brown onion, sliced
- 2 red chilies, seeded and chopped
- 1/2 C. teriyaki sauce
- 4 tbsp sweet chili sauce
- 17.5 oz. baby bok choy
- 7 oz. broccoli florets

Directions

1. Place a large skillet over medium heat. Heat in it the olive oil. Cook in the lamb strips in batches for 3 min.
2. Drain them and place them side. Heat the sesame oil in the same pan.
3. Cook in it the garlic with onion and chili for 3 min.
4. Stir in the lamb strips with teriyaki sauce, chili sauce, a pinch of salt and pepper.
5. Cook them for 2 min. Stir in the bok choy with broccoli and cook them for 3 to 4 min.
6. Serve your stir-fry warm with some rice.
7. Enjoy.

MUSHROOM
Teriyaki

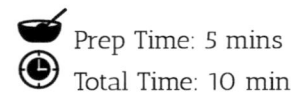

Prep Time: 5 mins
Total Time: 10 mins

Servings per Recipe: 4
Calories	74.3
Fat	3.7g
Cholesterol	0.0mg
Sodium	350.0mg
Carbohydrates	7.5g
Protein	3.8g

Ingredients

1 tbsp vegetable oil
1/2 lb. snow peas
8 ounces mushrooms, sliced

2 tbsps teriyaki sauce

Directions

1. Place a large pan over medium heat. Heat in it the oil.
2. Cook in it the mushroom with snow peas and a pinch of salt for 5 min.
3. Stir in the teriyaki sauce then serve them warm with some grilled or roasted meat.
4. Enjoy.

Korean Dinner (Chicken with Vegetables)

Prep Time: 15 mins
Total Time: 30 mins

Servings per Recipe: 4
Calories   705.2
Fat   9.8g
Cholesterol   36.3mg
Sodium   656.6mg
Carbohydrates   125.7g
Protein   24.7g

Ingredients

- 1 tbsp vegetable oil
- 12 asparagus spears, quartered
- 1 tbsp minced garlic
- 1/2 C. bell pepper, sliced
- 1/2 C. onion, diced
- 1 1/2 sliced mushrooms
- 1/2 lb. chicken breast, diced
- 3 C. prepared rice
- 1/4 C. dried cranberries
- 2 tsps cornstarch
- 3 tbsps teriyaki sauce
- 1/2 C. chicken broth

Directions

1. Place a large pan over medium heat. Heat in it the oil.
2. Cook in it the asparagus, peppers, onions, garlic and mushrooms for 4 to 6 min.
3. Stir in the chicken with cranberries, rice, a pinch of salt and pepper. Cook them for 6 min.
4. Get a mixing bowl: Whisk in it the cornstarch, teriyaki, and chicken broth.
5. Add the mixture to the pan and let it cook until the sauce becomes thick.
6. Serve your chicken pan warm.
7. Enjoy.

THURSDAY'S
Japanese Meatloaf Teriyaki

 Prep Time: 10 mins
Total Time: 1 hr 10 mins

Servings per Recipe: 6
Calories 357.6
Fat 17.1g
Cholesterol 168.7mg
Sodium 686.8mg
Carbohydrates 14.8g
Protein 34.2g

Ingredients

Meat
2 lbs. lean ground beef
2 eggs, lightly beaten
2 slices bread, soaked in water & squeezed dry
1/2 C. chopped green pepper
1 medium onion, finely chopped
1 tbsp parsley
1 tsp ginger
1 tbsp brown sugar

1 tbsp soy sauce
1 garlic clove, minced
Glaze
2 tbsps soy sauce
2 tbsps brown sugar
2 tbsps lemon juice

Directions

1. Get a large mixing bowl: Combine in it all the meatloaf ingredients.
2. Transfer the mixture to a greased bread pan and pat it down.
3. Bake it for 60 min.
4. Once the time is up, allow the meatloaf to rest for 6 min.
5. Place a heavy saucepan over medium heat: Whisk in it the lemon juice with brown sugar and soy sauce.
6. Cook them until the sugar dissolves and the sauce becomes slightly thick.
7. Pour the sauce all over the meatloaf then serve it warm.
8. Enjoy.

Braised Green Been Skillet

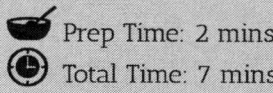

Prep Time: 2 mins
Total Time: 7 mins

Servings per Recipe: 4
Calories	77.4
Fat	0.2g
Cholesterol	0.0mg
Sodium	699.0mg
Carbohydrates	17.2g
Protein	3.9g

Ingredients

- 4 C. green beans, diced
- 1 large onion, diced
- 4 tbsps minced garlic
- 1/4 C. teriyaki sauce
- olive oil flavored cooking spray

Directions

1. Place a large skillet over medium heat. Grease it with a cooking spray.
2. Cook in it the green beans for 1 min. Stir in the onion and cook them for 3 min.
3. Stir in the garlic and cook them for 1 min.
4. Spoon the warm salad to a serving plate. Drizzle over it the teriyaki sauce then serve it.
5. Enjoy.

YUKI'S
Fish Cakes Teriyaki

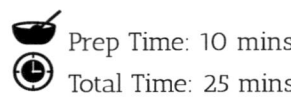

Prep Time: 10 mins
Total Time: 25 mins

Servings per Recipe: 6	
Calories	87.6
Fat	4.4g
Cholesterol	70.5mg
Sodium	205.6mg
Carbohydrates	8.2g
Protein	3.6g

Ingredients

1 (14 3/4 ounce) cans red sockeye, skin, and bones removed
1/2 C. dry breadcrumbs
3 green onions, thinly sliced
2 cloves garlic, finely chopped
1 tbsp orange juice

1 tbsp teriyaki sauce
2 large eggs, beaten
1 tbsp vegetable oil

Directions

1. Before you do anything, preheat the oven to 375 F.
2. Get a large mixing bowl: Mix in it the salmon, bread crumbs, garlic, orange juice, teriyaki sauce, a pinch of salt and pepper.
3. Add the eggs and combine them well. Form the mixture into 6 burgers.
4. Place a large skillet over medium heat. Heat in it the oil.
5. Cook in it the salmon cakes for 2 min on each side. Transfer them to a lined up baking tray.
6. Cook them for 11 min in the oven.
7. Serve your salmon cakes warm with the teriyaki sauce on the side.
8. Enjoy.

Tofu Teriyaki

Prep Time: 1 hr
Total Time: 2 hrs

Servings per Recipe: 4
Calories   147.9
Fat   4.9g
Cholesterol   0.0mg
Sodium   1021.1mg
Carbohydrates   17.1g
Protein   11.5g

Ingredients

- 1 lb. firm tofu, cut into bite-size pieces
- 1/4 C. soy sauce
- 3 tbsps rice vinegar
- 3 tbsps maple syrup
- 1/2 C. orange juice
- 2 tsps grated orange rind
- 1 tsp chopped gingerroot
- 2 cloves garlic, chopped
- 1/4 tsp dry mustard
- chopped coriander

Directions

1. Get a mixing bowl: Whisk in it the soy, vinegar, maple syrup, orange juice, orange rind, ginger, garlic, and mustard to make the marinade.
2. Place the tofu and in a large bowl and cover it with the marinade
3. Place it in the fridge and let sit for 60 min or overnight.
4. Before you do anything, preheat the oven to 375 F.
5. Drain the tofu pieces and place them in a roasting dish. Drizzle over the 1/2 C. of the remaining marinade.
6. Bake it for 60 min while stirring it every 22 min.
7. Serve your baked tofu warm.
8. Enjoy.

HIBACHI
Filets

Prep Time: 10 mins
Total Time: 25 mins

Servings per Recipe: 4
Calories	105.7
Fat	1.3g
Cholesterol	61.6mg
Sodium	240.4mg
Carbohydrates	5.0g
Protein	17.5g

Ingredients

4 white fish fillets
1/2 C. orange juice
2 green onions, chopped
1 tbsp teriyaki sauce
1 tsp ginger, grated

1 tsp cornflour
1 tbsp water

Directions

1. Get a mixing bowl: Whisk in it the orange juice, green onions, teriyaki sauce, ginger, a pinch of salt and pepper.
2. Add the fish fillets and let them sit for 60 min.
3. Place a heavy saucepan over medium heat.
4. Place in it the fish fillets with its marinade. Cook it until it starts boiling.
5. Put on the lid and let them cook until the fish is done. Drain it and place it aside.
6. Get a mixing bowl: Whisk in it the cornflour with water.
7. Add it to the sauce in the pan and simmer it until it becomes thick to your liking.
8. Adjust the seasoning of your teriyaki sauce then drizzle it over the fish fillets.
9. Serve them warm with some rice.
10. Enjoy.

Teriyaki Cauliflower Bowls

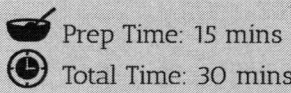
Prep Time: 15 mins
Total Time: 30 mins

Servings per Recipe: 8
Calories   40.5
Fat   0.1g
Cholesterol   0.0mg
Sodium   383.1mg
Carbohydrates   9.1g
Protein   1.6g

Ingredients

Teriyaki
- 2 tsps gingerroot, minced or grated
- 1 garlic clove, minced
- 3 tbsps water
- 1/3 C. low sodium soy sauce
- 1 tbsp honey
- 1/2 tsp onion powder
- 2 tbsps cornstarch
- 1/2 C. water

Veggies
- 2 C. cauliflower
- 2 celery ribs, sliced
- 2 medium carrots, peeled & julienned
- 1 medium zucchini, sliced

Directions

1. Place a heavy saucepan over high heat. Stir in 3 tbsp of water with garlic and ginger.
2. Put on the lid and let them cook for 2 min.
3. Stir in the soy sauce with honey and onion. Cook them for 2 min.
4. Get a mixing bowl: Whisk in it the cornstarch with water.
5. Add it to the saucepan and stir it until it becomes thick. Place it aside.
6. Place a large pan over high heat. Heat in it 1/2 C. of water.
7. Stir in the cauliflower with carrots and cook them for 3 min.
8. Stir in the celery with zucchini. Put on the lid and let them cook for 3 min.
9. Once the time is up, strain the veggies and transfer them to a serving plate.
10. Drizzle over the sauce and serve them warm.
11. Enjoy.

TERIYAKI
Sirloin

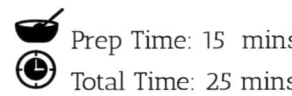

Prep Time: 15 mins
Total Time: 25 mins

Servings per Recipe: 6
Calories 54.1
Fat 2.3g
Cholesterol 0.0mg
Sodium 710.3mg
Carbohydrates 7.0g
Protein 1.1g

Ingredients

1/2 C. reduced sodium soy sauce
1/4 C. cider vinegar
2 tbsps brown sugar
2 tbsps chopped onions
1 tbsp canola oil
1 garlic clove, minced
1/2 tsp ground ginger
1/8 tsp pepper
2 lbs. beef top sirloin steaks

Directions

1. Get a zip lock bag: Combine in it the soy sauce with vinegar, sugar, onion, canola oil, garlic, ginger, salt, and pepper.
2. Cut the steaks into strips and add it to the bag. Seal it and shake them to coat.
3. Place it in the fridge for 3 h.
4. Before you do anything, preheat the grill and grease it.
5. Drain the beef strips and thread them onto skewers. Grill them for 4 to 5 min on each side.
6. Serve your grilled steak strips warm.
7. Enjoy.

Waldorf Teriyaki

Prep Time: 15 mins
Total Time: 35 mins

Servings per Recipe: 16
Calories   233.0
Fat   21.6g
Cholesterol   0.0mg
Sodium   253.0mg
Carbohydrates   8.2g
Protein   5.3g

Ingredients

- 4 C. walnut halves
- 3 tbsps sesame seeds
- 1/4 C. frozen orange juice concentrate, thawed
- 1/4 C. soy sauce
- 2 tbsps sesame oil
- 2 tbsps light brown sugar
- 2 tsps grated ginger
- 2 cloves garlic, minced
- 1/2 tsp crushed dried red chili

Directions

1. Before you do anything, preheat the oven to 350 F.
2. Cover a baking tray with a piece of foil. Arrange over the walnuts and toast them for 11 min.
3. Place them aside to cool down. Lower the oven heat for 300 F.
4. Place a skillet over medium heat. Cook in it the sesame seeds for 4 min until they become golden.
5. Transfer them to a bowl and place them aside.
6. Stir the orange juice concentrate, soy sauce, sesame oil, sugar, ginger, garlic and chilies in the same skillet.
7. Cook them until they start boiling. Stir in the walnuts and cook them until the sauce becomes thick.
8. Stir in the sesame seeds and mix them well. Spoon the mixture to the lined up tray and cook them for 9 min in the oven.
9. Allow your walnut candy to cool down completely then break it into pieces.
10. Store it in an airtight container and place it in a C.board until ready to serve.
11. Enjoy.

SAKURA'S 6-Ingredient Cutlets

Prep Time: 5 mins
Total Time: 25 mins

Servings per Recipe: 2
Calories	578.7
Fat	30.1g
Cholesterol	75.5mg
Sodium	2818.8mg
Carbohydrates	50.3g
Protein	30.4g

Ingredients

- 1/4 C. olive oil
- 1/3 C. honey
- 1/3 C. soy sauce
- 1/4 tsp ground pepper
- 2 garlic cloves
- 2 boneless skinless chicken breasts

Directions

1. Get a large mixing bowl: Mix in it the oil with honey, soy sauce, garlic, a pinch of salt and pepper.
2. Add to it the meat of your choice and let it sit for at least 2 h. Fry the breasts it in a skillet until fully done.
3. Enjoy.

Louisiana x Japanese Teriyaki

Prep Time: 5 mins
Total Time: 1 hr 5 mins

Servings per Recipe: 4
Calories	423.8
Fat	15.2g
Cholesterol	40.3mg
Sodium	1708.7mg
Carbohydrates	59.8g
Protein	12.5g

Ingredients

- 4 -6 sausages, your favorite kind
- 3/4 C. flour
- 1 tsp salt
- 1 1/2 tsps pepper
- 3/4 C. brown sugar
- 3 tbsps soy sauce
- 1/4 tsp lemon juice
- 1/2 tsp paprika
- 1/2 tsp cayenne
- 1/2 tsp garlic powder

Directions

1. Before you do anything, preheat the oven to 375 F.
2. Get a mixing bowl: Mix in it the flour with salt and pepper.
3. Dust the sausages with the flour mix and arrange them in a roasting pan.
4. Roast them in the oven for 22 min. Flip them and let them cook for an extra 20 min.
5. Get a mixing bowl: Mix in the brown sugar with soy sauce to get a thick paste.
6. Add the lemon juice with spices and combine them well. Brush the sausages with the sugar mixture.
7. Bake them for 11 min. Brush them one more time with the remaining sugar mixture and cook them for 11 min on the other side.
8. Serve your sausages warm.
9. Enjoy.

WHITE FISH
Teriyaki

Prep Time: 5 mins
Total Time: 15 mins

Servings per Recipe: 4
Calories	154.5
Fat	1.2g
Cholesterol	61.6mg
Sodium	2138.8mg
Carbohydrates	15.4g
Protein	20.0g

Ingredients

- 3/4 C. teriyaki marinade & sauce
- 2 tbsps brown sugar
- 1 tsp grated gingerroot
- 4 white fish fillets

Directions

1. Get a mixing bowl: Whisk in it the teriyaki marinade with brown sugar and gingerroot.
2. Get a zip lock bag: Place in it the fish fillet and pour over them 3/4 of the marinade.
3. Reserve the remaining 1/4 for later use. Seal the bag and let it sit for 35 min.
4. Before you do anything else, preheat the grill and grease it.
5. Drain the fish fillets and grill them for 4 to 5 min on each side.
6. Enjoy.

Teriyaki Brasileiro

Prep Time: 10 mins
Total Time: 30 mins

Servings per Recipe: 4
Calories   731.5
Fat   31.1g
Cholesterol   92.9mg
Sodium   1323.1mg
Carbohydrates   51.9g
Protein   58.7g

Ingredients

- 1/4 C. bottled teriyaki sauce
- 4 garlic cloves, crushed
- 1/4 tsp ground pepper
- 1 (2 lb.) flank steaks, cut into strips
- 3 bell peppers, quartered, seeded
- 1/2 lb. vermicelli
- 3 tbsps peanut oil
- 2 tbsps soy sauce
- 1 tsp oriental sesame oil
- 1 tsp grated ginger
- 1/4 tsp red pepper flakes
- 3 scallions, cut diagonally into slices

Directions

1. Get a roasting pan: Mix in it the teriyaki sauce, 2 cloves garlic, and the ground pepper.
2. Add the steaks and spoon over them the marinade. Let them sit for 30 min. Before you do anything else, preheat the oven broiler.
3. Drain the steak strips and thread them onto skewers. Arrange them in a roasting pan.
4. Thread the peppers onto skewers and add them to the roasting pan.
5. Pour over them the marinade. Broil them for 5 to 6 min on each side.
6. Prepare the vermicelli by following the instructions on the package.
7. Get a mixing bowl: Whisk in it the peanut oil, soy sauce, sesame oil, ginger, red pepper flakes, scallions, and remaining 2 cloves garlic.
8. Add the vermicelli and stir it to coat. Season it with a pinch of salt and pepper.
9. Serve your vermicelli warm with broiled steak and pepper.
10. Enjoy.

TERIYAKI
London Broil

🥣 Prep Time: 20 mins
🕐 Total Time: 35 mins

Servings per Recipe: 8
Calories   376.4
Fat   16.0g
Cholesterol   74.1mg
Sodium   385.7mg
Carbohydrates   29.3g
Protein   28.1g

Ingredients

2 lbs. London broil beef, cut into bite-size pieces
4 pita pockets
1 head lettuce
1 tbsp mayonnaise
Marinade
2 tbsps low sodium soy sauce
1/4 C. sesame oil
2 tbsps honey

Sauce
1 tbsp garlic powder
1 tbsp ground ginger
1 tbsp ground pepper
1 tsp celery salt
2 tbsps brown sugar
4 tbsps low sodium chicken broth
1 tbsp cornstarch

Directions

1. Get a zip lock bag: Combine in it the beef pieces with soy sauce, sesame oil, honey, a pinch of salt and pepper.
2. Seal the bag and place them aside for 60 min.
3. Slice the pita pockets in half and coat their inside with mayo.
4. Arrange in them the shredded lettuce and place them aside.
5. Place a hot pan over medium heat. Drain the beef pieces and cook them for 5 to 6 min.
6. Get a mixing bowl: Whisk in it the cornstarch with 1/4 C. of the beef marinade, garlic powder, ginger, pepper, brown sugar, broth, and salt. Pour the mixture over the beef pieces and cook them until it becomes thick.
7. Serve your glazed beef warm with some rice.
8. Enjoy.

Teriyaki Lunch Box (Chicken Wraps)

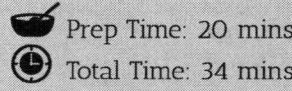 Prep Time: 20 mins
Total Time: 34 mins

Servings per Recipe: 6
Calories 415.0
Fat 7.8g
Cholesterol 43.8mg
Sodium 990.4mg
Carbohydrates 59.5g
Protein 25.7g

Ingredients

- 1/2 C. chopped walnuts
- 1 medium onion, sliced
- 1 lb. boneless skinless chicken breast, cut into strips
- 1 C. broccoli floret, blanched and drained
- 2 medium carrots, peeled, cut into matchsticks, blanched and drained
- 1/2 C. prepared teriyaki sauce
- 1/2 C. snow peas, halved on the diagonal, blanched and drained
- 6 10 inch 8-inch fat-free flour tortillas, warmed
- 2 C. hot cooked long-grain white rice

Directions

1. Place a large pan over medium heat. Toast in the walnuts for 2 min. Place it aside.
2. Place a pan over medium heat. Grease it with a cooking spray.
3. Cook in it the onion for 4 min. Stir in the chicken and cook them for 7 min.
4. Add the broccoli with carrots, snow peas, walnuts, teriyaki sauce, a pinch of salt and pepper.
5. Cook them for 3 min. Spoon the mixture into tortillas.
6. Top them with rice and fold them burrito style. Serve your sandwiches immediately.
7. Enjoy.

TOPPED
Teriyaki Chicken Breasts

 Prep Time: 45 mins
Total Time: 55 mins

Servings per Recipe: 4
Calories 348.5
Fat 4.9g
Cholesterol 65.8mg
Sodium 2201.8mg
Carbohydrates 48.5g
Protein 30.2g

Ingredients

1 lb. of boneless skinless chicken breast tenders
1 C. low sodium soy sauce
1 tbsp of grated gingerroot
3 garlic cloves, mashed and minced
2 limes, juice and zest, divided
1/2 C. honey
1 tbsp sesame oil
1 C. diced pineapple
1 jalapeno, seeded and halved
1/4 small onion
6 leaves basil
salt

Directions

1. Get a mixing bowl: Whisk in it the soy sauce, ginger, garlic, half of the lime juice and zest, honey, and sesame oil.
2. Stir in the chicken tenders and cover them. Place it in the fridge for 35 min.
3. Get a food processor: Combine in it the pineapple with basil, onion, and jalapeno.
4. Pulse them several times until they become finely chopped.
5. Before you do anything else, preheat the grill and grease it.
6. Drain the chicken tenders then season them with some salt and pepper.
7. Grill them for 5 to 6 min on each side. Serve them warm with pineapple salsa.
8. Enjoy.

Teriyaki Meat Brine

Prep Time: 10 mins
Total Time: 10 mins

Servings per Recipe: 1
Calories	581.8
Fat	36.3g
Cholesterol	0.0mg
Sodium	6046.1mg
Carbohydrates	56.2g
Protein	11.9g

Ingredients

- 1/4 C. soy sauce
- 1/4 C. grapefruit juice
- 2 tbsps olive oil
- 2 tbsps brown sugar
- 1 tbsp oyster sauce
- 1 1/2 tsps garlic powder
- 1/2 tsp ginger powder
- 1/2 tsp Chinese five spice powder
- 1/4 tsp Tabasco sauce

Directions

1. Get a zip lock bag: Combine in it all the ingredients with the meat of your choice.
2. Seal the bag and let it sit for 4 h. Cook it the way you desire.
3. Enjoy.

SHENZHEN
Stir Fry

Prep Time: 10 mins
Total Time: 18 mins

Servings per Recipe: 4
Calories   493.6
Fat   8.0g
Cholesterol   176.1mg
Sodium   2494.3mg
Carbohydrates   66.1g
Protein   37.5g

Ingredients

- 9 oz. fish fillets, cut into bite-size pieces
- 1 tbsp peanut oil
- 1 small red Spanish onion, sliced
- 1 small red capsicum, sliced
- 1 C. broccoli floret
- 9 oz. raw prawns
- 10.5 oz. fresh Hokkien noodles
- 3/4 C. teriyaki marinade

Directions

1. Place a large skillet over medium heat. Heat in it the oil.
2. Cook in it the onion with broccoli and capsicum for 3 min.
3. Stir in the shrimp with fish, a pinch of salt and pepper. Cook them for 3 min.
4. Stir in the noodles with teriyaki marinade. Cook them for 3 to 4 min.
5. Serve your stir-fry warm.
6. Enjoy.

Weeknight Burger Teriyaki

Prep Time: 10 mins
Total Time: 30 mins

Servings per Recipe: 5
Calories	227.9
Fat	10.1g
Cholesterol	101.2mg
Sodium	878.8mg
Carbohydrates	12.1g
Protein	21.1g

Ingredients

- 1 lb. lean ground beef
- 1/4 C. soy sauce
- 1/4 C. sugar
- 1 tbsp grated ginger
- 1 tbsp minced garlic
- 1 egg

Directions

1. Get a large mixing bowl: Mix in it all the ingredients.
2. Shape it into 5 burgers.
3. Before you do anything, preheat the grill and grease it.
4. Grill the burgers for 8 to 9 min on each side. Serve them warm.
5. Enjoy.

TERIYAKI
Meatball Sampler

Prep Time: 20 mins
Total Time: 30 mins

Servings per Recipe: 4
Calories	649.7
Fat	16.3g
Cholesterol	99.3mg
Sodium	1190.5mg
Carbohydrates	77.3g
Protein	47.0g

Ingredients

1 1/2 C. long grain rice
1 1/4 lbs. ground chicken
2 scallions, chopped
2 tbsps grated ginger
2 tbsps canola oil
1/2 lb. snow peas, halved crosswise
1 C. frozen shelled edamame, thawed
1/2 C. low sodium soy sauce
2 tbsps brown sugar

Directions

1. Prepare the rice by following the instructions on the package.
2. Get a mixing bowl: Mix in it the chicken, scallions, ginger, a pinch of salt and pepper.
3. Form the mixture into 16 meatballs.
4. Place a large pan over medium heat. Heat in it 1 tbsp of oil. Cook in it the meatballs for 12 min.
5. Drain them and place them aside. Stir the remaining oil in the same pan.
6. Stir in the edamame with peas, and a pinch of salt. Cook them for 3 min.
7. Stir in the meatballs.
8. Get a mixing bowl: Whisk in it the sugar with soy sauce. Stir it into the pan and cook them for 3 to 4 min.
9. Spoon the mixture over some rice then serve it warm.
10. Enjoy.

Alaskan Teriyaki

🥣 Prep Time: 2 hrs
🕒 Total Time: 2 hrs 10 mins

Servings per Recipe: 4
Calories   226.7
Fat   7.1g
Cholesterol   88.6mg
Sodium   122.5mg
Carbohydrates   4.2g
Protein   35.3g

Ingredients

- 1 1/2 lbs. salmon fillets
- 1 cedar plank
- 1 1/2 C. Yoshida gourmet sauce
- 1 tbsp sesame seeds
- 2 C. green onions, chopped

Directions

1. Place the cedar plank in a bucket of water and let it sit for 120 min.
2. Place the salmon fillets in a roasting dish. Pour over it the gourmet sauce and let them sit for 120 min.
3. Before you do anything else, preheat the grill and grease it.
4. Drain the fish fillets and grill them for 5 to 6 min on each side.
5. Garnish them with sesame seeds and green onions. Serve them warm.
6. Enjoy.

COUNTRY Vegetable Teriyaki

 Prep Time: 30 mins
Total Time: 40 mins

Servings per Recipe: 6
Calories   138.6
Fat   3.0g
Cholesterol   7.3mg
Sodium   1991.8mg
Carbohydrates   21.0g
Protein   10.7g

Ingredients

- 6 zucchini, sliced
- 6 yellow squash, sliced
- 2 (5 ounce) bottles teriyaki marinade
- 1/2 C. parmesan cheese, grated

Directions

1. Get a roasting dish: Stir in it the zucchini with squash, and teriyaki marinade
2. Cover the pan and let it sit for 12 h in the fridge.
3. Before you do anything, preheat the grill and grease it.
4. Drain the veggie slices and season them with a pinch of salt. Grill them for 2 to 3 min on each side.
5. Brush them with the marinade while cooking then serve them warm.
6. Enjoy.

Mr. Chow's Teriyaki Burgers

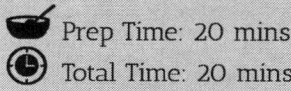

Prep Time: 20 mins
Total Time: 20 mins

Servings per Recipe: 6
Calories   447.9
Fat   19.3g
Cholesterol   77.1mg
Sodium   943.5mg
Carbohydrates   39.1g
Protein   28.1g

Ingredients

- 1 (8 ounces) can water chestnuts, drained and chopped
- 2 tbsps chopped green onions
- 1/3 C. teriyaki sauce
- 1 1/2 lbs. ground beef
- salt and pepper
- 7 split hamburger buns
- 14 slices tomatoes
- 7 lettuce leaves

Directions

1. Get a mixing bowl: Mix in it the teriyaki sauce, water chestnuts, onions, salt, and pepper.
2. Add the beef and combine them well. Form the mixture into 6 cakes.
3. Before you do anything, preheat the grill and grease it.
4. Grill the beef burgers for 7 to 9 min on each side. Serve them warm.
5. Enjoy.

LINGUINE
Teriyaki

🥣 Prep Time: 15 mins
🕐 Total Time: 30 mins

Servings per Recipe: 8
Calories   377.1
Fat   1.8g
Cholesterol   110.5mg
Sodium   1171.6mg
Carbohydrates   67.0g
Protein   23.6g

Ingredients

- 1 lb. cooked shrimp, 36 - 40 count
- 24 ounces broccoli
- 1/2 C. soy sauce
- 1/2 C. molasses
- 1/2 C. water
- 1 tsp Chinese five spice powder
- 1 tsp garlic powder
- 2 tbsps cornstarch
- 16 ounces linguine

Directions

1. To prepare the teriyaki sauce:
2. Place a heavy saucepan over medium heat: Stir in it the soy sauce, water, molasses, cornstarch, garlic powder and Chinese five spice.
3. Cook them until they become bubbly and thick.
4. To prepare the Pasta:
5. Bring a large salted saucepan of water to a boil. Cook in it the broccoli for 3 to 4 min.
6. Drain it and place it aside.
7. Get a large bowl: Place in it the shrimp and cover it with hot water. Let it sit for 6 min.
8. Cook the spaghetti by following the instructions on the package.
9. Place a large skillet over medium heat. Stir in it the broccoli with drained shrimp, teriyaki sauce, a pinch of salt and pepper.
10. Let them cook for 2 to 3 min. Stir in the pasta and stir them to coat.
11. Turn off the heat and put on the lid. Let them sit for 5 min.
12. Serve your pasta warm.
13. Enjoy.

Sesame Salmon

Prep Time: 15 mins
Total Time: 30 mins

Servings per Recipe: 2
Calories	905.9
Fat	22.9 g
Cholesterol	146.2 mg
Sodium	2265.8 mg
Carbohydrates	93.3 g
Protein	78.0 g

Ingredients

- 2 salmon fillets
- 2 heads pak choi
- 1 red pepper, sliced
- 1/2 tsp toasted sesame oil
- 1 garlic clove
- 1 tsp ginger
- 2 tsps coconut oil
- Himalayan salt and pepper
- 200 g brown rice
- 4 tbsps soy sauce
- 1 spring onion, chopped
- 1/2 chili, chopped
- 1 tsp ginger
- 1 garlic clove, minced
- 1 tbsp maple syrup
- 1 C. water
- 1 tsp cornflour

Directions

1. To prepare the teriyaki sauce:
2. Place a heavy saucepan over medium heat: Stir in it the soy sauce with spring onion, chili, ginger, garlic, maple syrup and ½ C. of water.
3. Cook them until they start boiling. Add the cornflour with water and mix them well.
4. Lower the heat and let the sauce cook until it becomes thick. Place it aside.
5. To prepare the salmon and veggies:
6. Place a large skillet over medium heat. Heat in it the coconut oil.
7. Sprinkle some salt and pepper all over the salmon fillets. Fry them for 3 to 4 min on each side. Drain them and place them over paper towels.
8. Place a heavy saucepan over medium heat. Heat it 1 tsp of coconut oil. Cook in it the ginger with garlic for 1 min. Stir in the peppers with pak choi, sesame oil, a pinch of salt and pepper. Let them cook for 4 min.
9. Prepare the rice by following the instructions on the package.
10. Spoon the rice to serving plates. Top them with veggies, salmon and teriyaki sauce.
11. Serve them right away. Enjoy.

TERIYAKI
Seafood Bowls

Prep Time: 20 mins
Total Time: 25 mins

Servings per Recipe: 3
Calories   269.7
Fat   10.6g
Cholesterol   190.9mg
Sodium   2698.0mg
Carbohydrates   18.8g
Protein   23.4g

Ingredients

1/2 C. teriyaki marinade, and sauce
2 tbsps sugar
water
1 lb. medium shrimp, peeled and deveined
2 tsps cornstarch
2 tbsps vegetable oil
hot cooked rice, about 4 C.
steamed vegetables

Directions

1. Get a mixing bowl: Whisk in it the teriyaki sauce with sugar. Reserve 3 tbsp of the sauce.
2. Get a zip lock bag: Combine in it the teriyaki sauce with shrimp, a pinch of salt and pepper.
3. Seal the bag and let them sit for 20 min.
4. Get a mixing bowl: Whisk in it 2/3 C. of water, 3 tbsp of the reserved marinade, and cornstarch.
5. Place a large pan over medium heat. Cook in it the shrimp for 4 min.
6. Stir in the cornstarch mixture and let them cook until the sauce becomes thick.
7. Serve your teriyaki shrimp warm with some rice and steamed veggies.
8. Enjoy.

Teriyaki Noodles

Prep Time: 3 hrs
Total Time: 3 hrs 25 mins

Servings per Recipe: 4	
Calories	544.4
Fat	9.3g
Cholesterol	65.8mg
Sodium	4854.0mg
Carbohydrates	72.7g
Protein	40.5g

Ingredients

- 1 lb. chicken tenderloins
- 1 1/3 C. teriyaki sauce, divided
- 2 tbsps peanut oil
- 2 carrots, sliced on the bias
- 1 C. small broccoli floret
- 2 celery ribs, sliced on the bias
- 1 (8 ounces) cans sliced water chestnuts, drained
- 1 medium onion, sliced
- 2 garlic cloves, minced
- 2 tbsps ginger, minced
- 2 green onions, sliced on the bias
- 8 ounces Japanese udon noodles

Directions

1. Get a mixing bowl: Stir in it 2/3 C. of teriyaki sauce with meat. Cover it and place it in the fridge for 4 h.
2. Before you do anything else, preheat the grill and grease it.
3. Drain the meat and grill it until it becomes cooked to your liking.
4. Place a large pan over medium heat. Heat in it the oil.
5. Cook in it the carrots with broccoli for 4 min. Stir in the celery with the onion and cook them for 3 min.
6. Stir in the water chestnuts, garlic, and ginger. Cook them for 2 min.
7. Prepare the noodles by following the instructions on the package.
8. Stir it into the pan and toss them to coat with 2/3 C. of teriyaki sauce and 1/2 C. of pasta water.
9. Lower the heat and let them cook until the sauce becomes thick.
10. Serve your teriyaki pasta beef warm.
11. Enjoy.

CHICKEN WING
Teriyaki

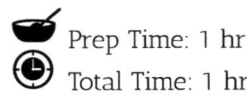
Prep Time: 1 hr
Total Time: 1 hr

Servings per Recipe: 8
Calories   1346.4
Fat   93.2g
Cholesterol   437.5mg
Sodium   1301.4mg
Carbohydrates   13.3g
Protein   106.9g

Ingredients

- 10 lbs. chicken wings
- 2 C. sweet and sour sauce
- 1/2 C. teriyaki sauce
- 1/4 C. sesame seeds

Directions

1. Before you do anything, preheat the oven to 450 F.
2. Place the chicken wings in a roasting dish. Coat them with a cooking spray.
3. Sprinkle over them some salt and pepper then toss them to coat. Place the pan in the oven and let them cook for 22 min.
4. Get a mixing bowl: Whisk in it the sweet and sour sauce with sesame seeds and teriyaki sauce.
5. Pour it all over the wings and stir them to coat. Place the pan back in the oven and cook them for 26 min.
6. Serve your chicken wings warm.
7. Enjoy.

Caribbean Teriyaki Sliders

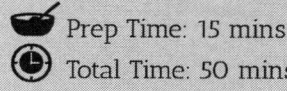

Prep Time: 15 mins
Total Time: 50 mins

Servings per Recipe: 2	
Calories	936.4
Fat	45.8g
Cholesterol	167.4mg
Sodium	2777.4mg
Carbohydrates	70.1g
Protein	59.9g

Ingredients

Teriyaki
pineapple juice
1/4 C. soy sauce
1 tbsp hoisin sauce
1/4 tsp sesame oil
3 tsps rice vinegar
3 tsps honey
2 garlic cloves, diced
Burger
3/4 lb. ground beef
1/4 C. of chopped cilantro
1 tsp dried red pepper flakes
2 green onions, diced
1 garlic clove, diced
salt and pepper
Toppings
4 slices swiss cheese
4 slices canned pineapple
4 buns, for sliders

Directions

1. To prepare the teriyaki sauce:
2. Place a heavy saucepan over medium heat.
3. Stir in it the garlic, soy sauce, Hoisin sauce, sesame oil, rice vinegar, pineapple juice, honey, and a pinch of salt.
4. Cook them until they start boiling. Lower the heat and let it cook until it becomes thick.
5. Turn off the heat and place it aside.
6. To prepare the burger:
7. Before you do anything, preheat the grill.
8. Get a large mixing bowl: Combine in it the beef, cilantro, red pepper flakes, green onions, salt, and garlic. Form the mixture into 4 burgers. Cook them for 5 to 6 min on each over the grill. Grill the pineapple slices for 1 to 2 min on each side until they become charred.
9. Cut your buns in half. Place the bottom halves on a serving plate.
10. Top them with some of the teriyaki sauce, grilled pineapple, burgers, a drizzle of teriyaki sauce and top buns. Serve your burgers immediately. Enjoy.

TERIYAKI
Pasta Salad

🥣 Prep Time: 2 hrs
⏱ Total Time: 2 hrs 5 mins

Servings per Recipe: 4
Calories 502.0
Fat 8.0g
Cholesterol 52.1mg
Sodium 2609.1mg
Carbohydrates 66.4g
Protein 37.2g

Ingredients

Marinade
1/2 C. soy sauce
1/2 C. sake
2 garlic cloves, minced
1-inch ginger, sliced into rounds
3 tbsps brown sugar
Dressing
2 scallions, sliced
2 garlic cloves, minced
2 tbsps rice vinegar
1/2 C. orange juice
2 tsps dark sesame oil
2 tbsps marinade, (first 5 ingredients)
Other Ingredients
1 lb. salmon
8 ounces soba noodles
4 ounces fresh spinach
3 carrots, scraped and cut into matchsticks

Directions

1. To prepare the marinade:
2. Place a heavy saucepan over medium heat. Stir in it all the marinade ingredients.
3. Cook them until they start boiling. Lower the heat and let it cook for 6 min.
4. Strain the marinade and place it aside to cool down. Reserve 2 tbsp of it for later use.
5. To prepare the dressing:
6. Get a mixing bowl:
7. Whisk in it the reserved 2 tbsp of the marinade. Add the dressing ingredients and combine them well.
8. Place it in the fridge until ready to serve.
9. To prepare the salad:
10. Get a roasting pan: Place in it the salmon fillets and cover it with 1/3 C. of the marinade.
11. Prepare the soba noodles by following the instructions on the package. Add to it the carrots while cooking it.
12. Before you do anything, preheat the oven broiler.

13. Drain the salmon fillets and place them on a baking tray.
14. Broil them for 4 to 5 min on each side while brushing them with the remaining marinade.
15. Arrange the spinach leaves on serving plates.
16. Stir the noodles with carrots into the dressing. Season them with a pinch of salt.
17. Spoon the mixture over the spinach layer and top them with the broiled salmon. Serve them warm.
18. Enjoy.

SPICY
Japanese Pizza

 Prep Time: 5 mins
Total Time: 25 mins

Servings per Recipe: 1
Calories	446.1
Fat	27.3g
Cholesterol	123.3mg
Sodium	1502.0mg
Carbohydrates	11.1g
Protein	36.5g

Ingredients

- 1/2 lb. ground beef
- 1/2 onion, minced
- 2 tbsps teriyaki sauce
- pre-shredded mozzarella cheese
- 1/2 jalapeno
- 2 -3 bread

Directions

1. Before you do anything, preheat the oven to 350 F.
2. Place a skillet over high heat. Brown in it the beef for 4 to 5 min.
3. Discard the excess grease. Stir in the onion and cook them for 3 min.
4. Lower the heat and stir in the teriyaki sauce. Let them cook for 3 to 4 min until the liquid evaporates.
5. Place the bread loaves on a baking tray. Spread over them the beef mixture.
6. Sprinkle the mozzarella cheese on top followed by jalapeno.
7. Bake your pizzas for 11 min then serve them warm.
8. Enjoy.

Ginger Teriyaki Nuts

Prep Time: 10 mins
Total Time: 10 mins

Servings per Recipe: 1
Calories   1025.4
Fat   92.2g
Cholesterol   0.0mg
Sodium   2479.1mg
Carbohydrates   31.7g
Protein   32.9g

Ingredients

- 1/4 C. soy sauce
- 3 tbsps raw agave nectar
- 3 tbsps sesame oil
- 1 tbsp ginger
- 2 C. whole raw almonds

Directions

1. Get a food processor: Place in it the soy sauce with sesame oil and ginger. Blend them smooth.
2. Get a mixing bowl: Stir in it the sauce with almonds. Serve them with some bread.
3. Enjoy.

TERIYAKI
Oysters

 Prep Time: 35 mins
Total Time: 45 mins

Servings per Recipe: 4
Calories 2337.1
Fat 242.3g
Cholesterol 90.2mg
Sodium 968.5mg
Carbohydrates 32.4g
Protein 15.9g

Ingredients

- 1 dozen oyster, shucked
- 1/2 C. tempura flour
- 1 C. orange juice
- 1/4 C. sweet gherkins
- 4 garlic cloves, smashed
- 2 tbsps teriyaki sauce
- 1 C. mayonnaise
- 1 tsp olive oil
- 4 C. canola oil

Directions

1. Place a large saucepan over medium heat. Stir in it the garlic with olive oil.
2. Cook them for 1 min. Drain the garlic and place it aside.
3. Stir in the orange juice with pickle juice. Cook them until they reduce by 2/3.
4. Turn off the heat and let the sauce cool down for 30 min.
5. Get a mixing bowl: Mix in it the oysters liquid with mayonnaise. Place it aside.
6. Place a large skillet over medium heat. Heat in it the canola oil.
7. Toss the oysters in tempura flour then season them with a pinch of salt and pepper.
8. Cook them for 2 to 3 min until they become brown. Serve your oyster fries with mayonnaise and orange sauce.
9. Enjoy.

Hawaiian Teriyaki Ribs

Prep Time: 15 mins
Total Time: 35 mins

Servings per Recipe: 4
Calories	346.6
Fat	26.6g
Cholesterol	61.0mg
Sodium	877.4mg
Carbohydrates	29.7g
Protein	1.4g

Ingredients

- 4 rib eye steaks
- 1 tbsp oil
- 1 1/2 tsps salt
- 1/4 C. McCormick's Montreal Brand steak seasoning
- 2/3 C. Kikkoman Teriyaki Baste and Glaze with Honey and Pineapple
- 1 pineapple
- 1 salt
- 1/2 C. unsalted butter, melted

Directions

1. Before you do anything, preheat the oven to 500 F.
2. Line up a baking sheet with foil. Grease it with oil.
3. Sprinkle some salt and steak seasoning all over the rib steaks. Let them sit for 12 min.
4. Coat the steaks with teriyaki baste and glaze. Arrange them on the lined sheet and bake them for 7 min.
5. Place a large pan over medium heat. Coat the pineapple rings with butter.
6. Cook them in the hot pan for 1 min on each side.
7. Serve your broiled steaks warm with pineapple rings.
8. Enjoy.

MUSHROOM Teriyaki

Prep Time: 15 mins
Total Time: 5 hrs 15 mins

Servings per Recipe: 4
Calories 88.4
Fat 3.8g
Cholesterol 0.0mg
Sodium 515.0mg
Carbohydrates 11.8g
Protein 3.4g

Ingredients

1 tbsp olive oil
1 lb. portabella mushroom, stemmed and quartered
2 tbsps brown sugar
2 tbsps soy sauce
1/2 tsp dry mustard
1/2 tsp ground ginger

Directions

1. Grease a slow cooker with olive oil. Stir in it all the ingredients.
2. Season them with a pinch of salt and pepper. Put on the lid and let them cook for 6 h on low or 3 h on high.
3. Serve your teriyaki mushroom stew warm with some rice.
4. Enjoy.

Beef Teriyaki

Prep Time: 24 hrs
Total Time: 24 hrs 25 mins

Servings per Recipe:	8
Calories	336.3
Fat	12.4g
Cholesterol	110.5mg
Sodium	2105.7mg
Carbohydrates	15.5g
Protein	39.2g

Ingredients

- 3 -5 lbs. tri-tip roast
- 1 C. soy sauce
- 1/2 C. sugar
- 4 -6 garlic cloves, chopped
- 2 tsps grated ginger
- 3 green onions, chopped
- 1 tsp black pepper

Directions

1. Get a zip lock bag; combine in it all the ingredients.
2. Let them marinate for 25 h.
3. Before you do anything, preheat the grill and grease it.
4. Grill the steaks for 6 to 8 min on each side. Serve them warm.
5. Enjoy.

20 MINUTE Weeknight Teriyaki Fish

Prep Time: 10 mins
Total Time: 18 mins

Servings per Recipe: 3
Calories   418.7
Fat   2.0g
Cholesterol   124.6mg
Sodium   4199.4mg
Carbohydrates   38.0g
Protein   59.4g

Ingredients

3/4 C. soy sauce
1/2 C. sugar
1 tsp grated gingerroot
1 garlic clove, peeled and crushed
1 tbsp sake

1 1/2 lbs. fish fillets

Directions

1. Get microwave pan: Mix in it the soy sauce with sugar, gingerroot, garlic, and sake.
2. Stir in the fish fillets with a pinch of salt and pepper. Put on the lid and let them sit for 35 min.
3. Once the time is up, remove the lid and microwave the fish fillets for 8 min on high.
4. Serve them warm with some rice.
5. Enjoy.

Printed in Great Britain
by Amazon